A Groundbreaking Approach to Customer-Centric Messaging Strategy

YOUR MESSAGING SUCKS

Become the Brand Your Customers Love

KIM R. DONLAN

Your Messaging Sucks: Become the Brand Your Customers Love

Copyright 2023 Kim R. Donlan

All rights reserved. No part of this book may be reproduced or used in any manner without the prior written permission of the copyright owner, except for the use of brief quotations in a book review.

To request permissions, contact the author: KDonlan@RedSwan5.com

Printed in the United States of America.
First paperback edition February 2023

Cover and layout design by
G Sharp Design, LLC
www.gsharpmajor.com

Copy editing by
Hugh Barker

Author photo by
Hornick Rivlin Studio

ISBN 979-8-9866530-0-6 (hardcover)
ISBN 979-8-9866530-1-3 (paperback)
ISBN 979-8-9866530-2-0 (ebook)

Disclaimer: This book is based on working with hundreds of people over thirty years. Client stories and examples were manufactured—combining different people, brands, and projects. Identities of people and circumstances described are purely coincidental. Neither the publisher nor author shall be liable for any loss of profit or any other commercial damages, including but not limited to special, incidental, consequential, personable, or other damages.

For Liza, Ella, and Ruby—

You are everything.
I love you.

Contents

Introduction

When I help create a messaging strategy, the people in the room directly affect the type of messaging and strategy that emerges. The people – their insights, experiences, and willingness to listen (or not) – make the messaging and positioning unique (or not). Customers aren't in the room, but are represented in reports and commentary that can be interpreted in a way that supports the brand's perspective of what they believe their customers value.

I have always approached marketing from the perspective of a customer. It comes from a lifetime of being an outsider, and a career encompassing diverse roles. I learned the hard way – through surprising failures and unexpected successes that I didn't always understand. As a CMO for tech start-ups, a digital agency leader, entrepreneur, academic, and pioneer in messaging, technology, and strategy, I specialized in the infancy, early stage, and pivot points of businesses, when a new market needed to be found. In each role, my job was to uncover what the brand could be and connect it to customers who would love and value it.

Getting a brand to agree on what they truly are and finding the customers who love them is not easy. It means giving up what the brand has often spent much time and energy believing, and telling the founders and marketers they are not what customers want. Brands must know what the consumer thinks and feels before they buy: how the products and services connect on an emotional level – and the underlying habit that can trigger a connection. But no one teaches brand folks how to do it. And there usually remain differing views within the brand that interfere with its ability to engage.

This book shares the techniques perfected over 30 years of being curious about how to bring the customer into the room, and building a new messaging strategy process around them. I offer workshops, exercises, and frameworks that help brands approach messaging with a better method, allowing them to shift their strategy and align their messaging for the best customers. I provide techniques to help brands see how customers think, feel, and behave in ways that will change the brand experience. I also deliver frameworks that force brands to look at themselves from the customer's perspective. Often, this approach will uncover new revenue streams and establish a more prosperous, competitive position.

The Problem with Messaging

Like people, brands want to be heard. To be understood, and valued. To be shown appreciation with purchases, loyalty, and reputation. After all the work on market research, product development, brand strategy, lead generation programs, and campaigns, it is still possible that no one is listening. No one wants you. You are left dumbfounded. It can be frustrating when prospects, consumers, or investors don't get you. When your marketing efforts don't connect with the people you believe need you, you can feel like you have failed. However, you didn't fail; you just followed a marketing process that failed you.

The gap between what you think you are offering and what your audience believes you are offering creates a messaging problem. It is hard to recognize the fact that you have a messaging problem, because it initially appears to be an implementation or execution issue. When prospects aren't buying, it is often blamed on marketing not providing the right leads. If customers flock to a competitor for products that you offer, we point to the product development team (and marketing team). If new prospects abandon the sales process, we fiddle with the user experience. Then, when all else fails, we point to the individuals, departments, or agencies involved. Indeed, it is the stressed marketer, lazy salesperson, inept product developer, founder's lack of vision, agencies that didn't get you, or the stupid consumer. We never work on the core problem – this is the fact that the way we create messaging is broken.

Messaging strategy requires you to look at your offer from the customer's point of view. Messaging is the connection – the bridge between the brand's view of themselves and the customer's understanding. To work well, messaging must be audience-centric and match the audience's words, emotions, perspective, and mindset. Messaging is the adhesive that allows the value exchange to stick. Yet we do it last.

Current approaches to market research, SWOT analysis, persona development, customer journeys, product development, prototyping, positioning, beta testing, and brand strategy are all steps from the brand's perspective. Yes, we ask potential target customers questions. And there may be good feedback from the beta; but are you listening? Can you hear if you are making mistakes in your approach? The answer is usually no.

Whether you are a VC-backed start-up, an entrepreneur seeking funding or customers, or a more prominent firm that has hit a wall, a new website, campaign, or social program will not solve a problem with a flawed process. Messaging developed at the very end of the marketing process should never be the first time you see your product or service from the only viewpoint that matters – your customers' viewpoint.

In this time of customer-centricity and engagement-based competitiveness, we must ensure that we create a brand strategy that connects with customers. The customer perspective must be your only lens. A new messaging strategy and process can help you reach the people you want. If you follow the lessons in this book, you and your product or service will be more than desired. You'll be loved.

Section 1

Customer-Centric Messaging Strategy

Chapter 1

What Is It?

Key Idea

If you can't describe your brand in a single sentence, you have not done the long, hard work required to create a clear statement that immediately tells the audience what you are. Getting to a clear message takes time, sacrifice, and giving in to the idea that your brand is what your audience believes it is. This hard work is often ignored for two excellent, but often fatal reasons. The first is that you believe that, once your potential audience sees your brilliant product or service, it will be crystal-clear that it is better than the competitors. The second is that your possible audience is enormous – many people could use your fantastic product and service. Both belief systems result in painful loss and, sometimes, business or product failure.

A contributing factor to broken go-to-market messaging is the inability to see the brand from a customer perspective. As an expert in your chosen field, surely you know what the customer needs better than they do. You understand the industry, see the pain points, have analyzed the competition, and are secure in your assessment of how you fit into the market. You KNOW this world. You studied the problems and have a better way. You don't just fix the problem. You are a far better choice than what is currently available. The customer feedback – if you received any – confirmed all that you know. You listened to your friends, colleagues, and partners. You heard such positive sentiments that you went full throttle into the funding pitch, new customer presentation, campaign development, new website, and perhaps even a minimum viable product. However, when asked what you provide, the words sputter out endlessly, and a quick sentence turns into rambling as you try to convey, what it is that you do. It gets uncomfortable pretty quickly.

When your brand is indescribable, it isn't a good thing. It means there is nothing for your audience to hold onto, and you risk not having a single idea that is easily communicated. Great strategic messaging requires you to avoid becoming a slightly better version of something already in the market. Great messaging requires you to dare to be something different: to see yourself from the customer's perspective – and not every customer – but the ones that truly need you. This is not to say that you will be the SAME for each customer. Each customer will experience your brand as they need to and co-create the meaning of what you do for them. But initially, you need to be the brand they want. And for that to happen, you must describe what you are from their perspective.

Explaining what you do takes hard work, sacrifice, and precision. It is difficult to give up your perspective, and see it entirely from another view. It takes sacrifice to hone in on the initial idea that will resonate with your customer. Then it takes precision to find the exact places where you have an opportunity to connect. You must release the idea of being ALL things to ALL customers in order to become one great thing to the right customer. Once you have built the connection, you can grow – but first, you need to describe what you do in a way that gets people to listen. Doing the hard work now could very well save your brand.

What Is Wrong with Current Methods?

While you need to create value to sustain a business, the traditional development of a value proposition, brand promise, and initial pitch is formulated from the brand's perspective and not the customer's point of view. Many existing exercises, processes, and templates are set up for the brand to determine who *they* are, not to consider the customer's perspective.

The existing tools used by marketers, consultants, and agencies restrict the perceptions and ideas to the people involved in the room during the brand strategy process. The people in the room make decisions about the brand, and they hold the power to shape the messaging to their liking and discount any challenge to the customer or market feedback. The people in the room and the existing tools create an echo chamber, leading to a flawed go-to-market strategy. Confronted with simple questions like, "Tell me about your brand" are met with an ever-changing description of the brand – you just can't get a concise answer.

To shift the focus to a customer's perspective, you change how you get to the value proposition. You put the customer's perspective in the room. You create a construct that sees the customer's point of view as equal to or more important than the founders.' You start by asking the question your customer will be thinking: "What is it?" Then you challenge yourself and your team to answer it, as *they* need to understand it.

When you ask, "What is it?", most people answer the question, "What do you do?" By contrast, answering the question, "What is it?" compels you to hover above the features, benefits, and results – to stretch yourself to describe what it is in such a way that your customers will get it. When you are asked, "What is it?" is your initial response something that could be used to describe any competitor in your industry, or is it a jargon-rich line that might make you look brilliant – but rather lonely since no one gets you?

What if you asked your colleagues, customers, or shareholders? Would they provide an answer you'd recognize, or would it seem like a completely different brand? Could they describe what makes you unique? Could they represent your value?

"What is it?" is a deceptively simple question. The answer sometimes relies on such a slight nuance that it is often overlooked or thought of as too insufficient to matter. But it's there. "What is it?" can't be answered by technical terms that customers can't appreciate. It can't be so vague that it is meaningless. The answer requires a clear statement immediately telling your audience what you are to them.

When Do You Need to Address This?

You know you need to address this question when there is a disconnect between the way customers or prospects describe you and the way you describe yourself. You might be getting referrals for work you don't perform or losing assignments you should get. It may be that your funding pitch gets interrupted in the first three minutes as the potential investors grapple with what makes you fundable. Alternatively, maybe every company you pitch to reflects something completely different, even when you have delivered the same slide deck. These tell-tale signs show you have developed a brand strategy based on a flawed process that only considers your perspective.

Sales Messaging Alignment

Frustration escalates as marketing and sales try to understand why lead generation isn't working. Potential new customer deals are stalled. When you listen to what the sales reps say, they describe the company so differently that potential customers are confused. Or they still don't know all that your company offers even after several meetings.

Brand Refresh

When the initial go-to-market strategy falters, there is a justifiable call for a brand refresh. Unfortunately, this will lead to disappointment if the approach only considers the brand's point of view. A brand refresh can be a design and user experience exercise that hopes to address problems in sales, positioning, or revised product architecture. However, if the messaging remains focused on the brand's perspective, it will not solve the fundamental issues.

Start-up Beta Customer Pitch

During the funding elevator pitch, your description starts to sputter, and you can't adequately articulate what you offer. You begin to lose confidence and wonder if your valuable idea will ever see the light of day. This holds for the important alpha customers you desperately need, and you can't seem to express how you will solve the problem they have.

Why Doing This Now Will Get You a Better ROI

Customers want to feel comfortable. Remember, they are searching for an instant connection – confirmation they are interacting with the right brand. The faster the audience feels confident that their needs will be met, the more receptive they will be to you and your goals. Confusion breeds distrust, insecurity, and frustration. If you and the audience disagree on "what it is," there is no trust in the relationship.

Brands that can't easily articulate what they are miss revenue opportunities and will take far too long to close deals which should be relatively easy. The ability to explain "what it is" can have a dramatic impact on your bottom line.

The ability to answer the question "What is it?" will increase the quality of your lead flow. You can expect that a clear message will provide a more substantial alignment with marketing-qualified leads. The more precise you can be about what you sell, the more easily customers can self-select what products and services they need from you. Additionally, your sales or funding presentations will advance further in the process. Again, once you eliminate the confusion, your potential customers and funders will focus on your fit in the industry.

The following workshop and exercises are often the first time everyone comes together to discuss what it is. Having a listening exercise that shifts you, from the slow path to nowhere, to a more straightforward approach will lead to faster growth. The outcome will be features and benefits that make you, well… you. You'll be able to make small changes in your campaigns and sales presentations to accelerate the marketing of qualified leads (MQL).

How to Fix It - Workshop and Exercises

What Is It?

The first workshop establishes the groundwork for a new way of marketing. Get set for imperfect – new beginnings are always wobbly. The old talking points, positioning statements, target audiences, and client stories will be revisited, regurgitated, and debated. Expect clashes and hard conversations left unresolved in this workshop. This session will be the first time all you know, and your colleagues know is discussed openly in one place, for all to see. Countless times, when I have facilitated this workshop, the participants have marveled at how much of a cathartic experience it is. It is the first opportunity for everyone to unpack the internalization of previous failed attempts to describe the brand. The workshop brings to the surface the tension, frustrations, and the release of finally being able to discuss the problem within a context and methodology that will allow for a positive resolution.

The first exercise focuses on information gathering and categorizing the current belief system. The first aim is to bring all your participants' beliefs to the surface before transitioning to customer-centric messaging. The second exercise will make the initial attempt at alignment with the brand's philosophy. There is NO attempt to resolve the question, "What is it?" However, the participants will leave the workshop with a mindset to continue thinking about the discussion and a second scheduled meeting to refine the results of this exercise. You need participants to gain a new awareness of how the different brand-centric perspectives interfere with progress.

Exercise 1.1: What Is It?

Timeframe

45 minutes

Focus

Information Gathering | Categorization

Participant Instructions

This is the first attempt to define a fundamental question. It will be messy, and you won't reach a final conclusion, but we will begin to resolve what we think we are and get to what kind of customer messaging will allow us to move forward.

Facilitator Instructions

This exercise is about listening. You'll need to be open to nuances that can lead to a breakthrough. The more senior members – like founders or chief technology officers – can have biases that prevent them from seeing things any differently. Encourage the junior participants to share their statements even if they believe they will be similar to what the group's more senior members would say.

Don't transcribe the entire sentence as you transition the ideas from individual participants to the whiteboard or PPT templates. Just pull in the critical items from the sentence. You're building a grid to keep things that seem related in the same column.

Step-by-Step Guideline

The pace and timeframe may be shorter or longer than suggested. Use this as a guide and, if necessary, break it into multiple sessions.

5 minutes

1. Each participant spends 5 minutes writing a single-sentence answer to the question "What is it?" Instruct them to write one sentence on each card/post-it provided.
2. It is essential to allow the participants to write multiple sentences – and ask them to keep all the versions they produce.

15 minutes

3. After 5 minutes, you can begin with any participant, asking them to read one of their cards. Two actions must happen:
   - Transcribe the statement on the wall (whiteboard/ larger post-it sheet or use the PowerPoint template)
   - As you read the cards, place them in the middle of the table.
4. Ask other participants if they had something similar.
   - If they do, have the participant add it to the same pile in the middle of the table
   - If there is an important nuance, do not add it. Write the new statement on the whiteboard under the previous one.

♥ **Note**: *This process will quickly turn into a discussion. Allow this to happen with the caveat of agreeing on what is essential to add to the board for further dialogue or is similar enough that it's the same statement.*

5. One by one, single statements are transcribed to the wall and either delegated to an existing pile or deemed worthy of being added to a new stack.

15 minutes

6. Encourage discussion on the common elements identified. Look for small agreements and similarities that participants cannot categorize as being the same. There may be nuances that are not well articulated, but instinctively, the participants know there is a crucial differentiator in those nuances. Connect these visually with big circles and lines, showing what everyone agrees is the same answer.

10 minutes

7. It is time to *prioritize the statements*. Which statements are powerful differentiators – because you have new technology, process, approach, or expertise? You are looking for what you do better. It may be that the list shows some similarities to competitors, but the order or combination is a deciding factor. Ask participants to agree on which items on the whiteboard/wall are essential. You can bold, highlight, or circle these powerful differentiators. There should be no more than three.

♥ **Note:** *There will be some pushback as participants become uncomfortable with prioritizing and raise objections based on their understanding of the target audience. You may hear something to the effect of, "Well, the answer depends on whom we are selling to." Respond by saying that the audience is what you believe represents your best customer and what would be most important to that best customer.*

8. Leave the straggling statements where they are. As with the main statements, ask whether the stragglers have common elements. Combine with existing ideas and connect or collapse them. If they remain stragglers, ask participant(s) to explain them further – it is a discussion, not a debate. Sometimes these outliers are critical. Sometimes they are false claims. So let them dangle there until you know. At this stage, you can move on to Exercise 2, but keep a record the outliers so you can revisit them later.

What To Do Next

Now

- Photograph the whiteboard as it is! Since you'll be moving things around, keeping a record of the original session is important.
- Collect the cards in the middle. There may be discarded items that prove to be worth remembering later.

Later

- Add the critical features as column heads along the top of the grid
    - You will begin reorganizing the content from the "What is it?" feedback with features from your current marketing material in a smaller team or just by yourself. Add your current features as column headers. If there are several options for the key features – select the one that makes the most sense for you.
    - You should also add critical features on which the industry generally competes (pull from an analyst or benchmark reports)

- Move the workshop statements, so they align with the features
  - Highlight the prioritized statements so you can see how they relate to the features

Exercise 1.1: Templates and Examples

- **Figure 1:** "What Is It?" Grid Template
- **Figure 2:** Example of "What is it?" for an Online Pet Supply, Training, and Certification Website for Working Service Dogs
- **Figure 3:** Example of "What is it?" for an Online Store for Pet Supply, Training, and Certification for Working Service Dogs with Marketing Features Added

Figure 1: "What Is It?" Grid Template

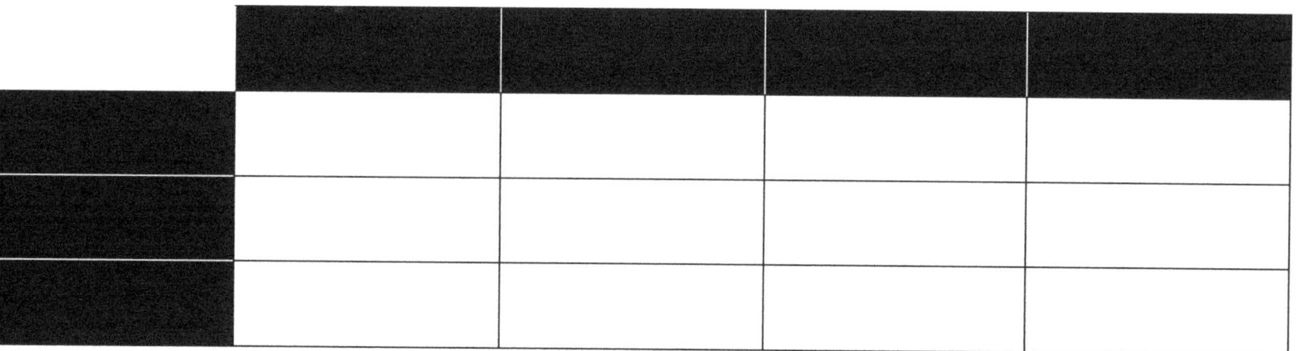

Figure 1: You are capturing participants' comments and beginning to categorize the feedback into groups of similar content. Each column should include content that may be the same but just described slightly differently or at least closely related. Ask the participant where they think the comments should go. You can draw a grid on a whiteboard or use a PowerPoint template. Do not write in the top row or far left column. You'll need this space for Exercise 1.2

Figure 2: Example of "What is it?" for an Online Pet Supply, Training, and Certification Website for Working Service Dogs

	Get professional (**certified**) Emotional Support Animal Training	Healthy (**natural ingredients**)	Official harness with handle (**service animal**)	Clicker	Which diagnosis (**conditions**) qualify?	Trusted certification (**authentic**)	**Official requirements for service animal status**
	Trusted training (not scam/ fraudulent sites)	Clicker training (**reward-motivation**) treats	Patches (people and dog)	Treat bags	Understand Therapy dog vs **Service dog requirements**	Qualifying conditions (physical and mental health diagnosis)	**Trusted** as of U.S. Service and Support Animal Registration Database (**only source or compliance**)
	Convenient online training is as effective as in-person (and less expensive)	Organic vegetable (meat-free) snacks	Fast (**timely**) access to photo **IDs/certification (digital)**	Leashes	Improve travel experience	**Less expensive than in-person**	**Process for legal assistance** (help if rights are violated)
	Activities dogs need to perform	Tasty Treats	Dog packs **(medical supply packs)**		**Medical diagnosis documents** (Doctors' letters)	Activities dogs need to perform	(Free) **access to National Database** (compliance?)

Figure 2: Here is an example of an ecommerce site. Notice the items in parenthesis (). These are responses with similar meanings but no agreement among the participants as to whether they were one or the other. Be prepared to highlight instances where there are different definitions of what appears to be the same thing. For example, is "timely" the same as "fast," and does "trusted" mean "certified," or is 'diagnosis' the same as 'conditions? Watch for words or phrases used by competitors that don't work for your brand. Having a competitor's narrative on your site doesn't help your brand differentiate itself.

Note: The bolded text is the attributes deemed to be a high priority – the key differentiators.

Figure 3: Example of "What is it?" for an Online Store for Pet Supply, Training, and Certification for Working Service Dogs with Marketing Features Added

Features pulled from marketing materials	Training	Quality Treats	Harness/Vests IDs	Toys & Supplies	Working Dog Qualification	Certification	Registration	Is this important?
Priority 1	Get professional (**certified**) Emotional Support Animal Training	Clicker training (**reward-motivation**) treats	Fast (**timely**) access to photo **IDs/certification (digital)**	Clicker	Qualifying conditions (physical and mental health diagnosis)	Trusted certification (**authentic**)	**Official requirements for service animal status**	Improve travel experience
Priority 2	**Convenient online training** is as effective as in-person (and less expensive)	Healthy (**natural ingredients**)	Official harness with handle **(service animal)**	Treat bags	**Medical diagnosis documents** (Doctors' letters)	Qualifying conditions (physical and mental health diagnosis)	**Trusted** as of U.S. Service and Support Animal Registration Database (**only source or compliance**)	(Help if rights are violated)
Priority 3	**Trusted training** (not scam/ fraudulent sites)	Organic vegetable (meat-free) snacks	Dog packs **(medical supply packs)**	Leashes	**Understand** Therapy dog vs **Service dog requirements**	**Less expensive than in-person**	**Process for legal assistance**	
			Patches (people and dog)			Activities dogs need to perform	(Free) **access to National Database** (compliance?)	

Figure 3: Here is an example of taking the existing feature from the marketing or presentation materials and adding it as headers. The statements under each heading are then shuffled into the most appropriate column and prioritized. You can already see some interesting messaging gaps. Some content was removed when it didn't make sense as part of the feature. Any content that didn't seem to fit in an existing column was added to a new column

Exercise 1.2: Are You Close To Your Purpose?

Timeframe

20 minutes

Focus

Alignment

Participant Instructions

This is the first attempt to check in on your purpose or mission statement. Some brands have mission statements, and some have a purpose. Whichever you have, it's time to bring it forward. We are not going to change the brand's purpose or mission statement at this time. This exercise verifies if the priorities listed in the "What is it?" grid match the purpose. In other words, this is the first pass at how aligned you are.

Facilitator Instructions

In this exercise, you will indicate which items on the grid fit with the purpose/mission and are a priority by adding an asterisk. You need a way to represent which items are most critical visually. It is the first attempt to prioritize what is it and what it is not.

Step-by-Step Guideline

This exercise can take 20 minutes, depending on the level and energy the discussion involves. If you are well aligned, it may be quick. If not, it may take longer to identify where you are out of alignment. A big distance between the purpose and what you actually do can take longer and lead to a new session where you focus on reworking your purpose.

20 minutes

1. Write or project the purpose/mission statement. Read it to the participants.
2. One by one, read the prioritized list of the items from the "What is it?" exercise grid and ask participants if they can see a connection between the answer and the purpose/mission statement.
3. If the item is deemed a priority AND fits within the purpose/mission statement, add an asterisk next to the item. Continue until all prioritized items are complete.
4. For the outlier features, ask if they fit in the purpose/mission statement.
   - If an attribute differs from the other descriptions, is deemed a priority, AND fits the purpose/mission statement, add it to the grid.
   - If it differs from the other statements and is deemed a priority BUT does not fit the purpose mission statement, set it aside.

♥ **Note:** *If most of the grid content describes what you do but doesn't match the purpose or mission, it may be that the purpose/mission statement is outdated, and it's time to take a look at that.*

What To Do Next

Now

- Photograph the whiteboard/wall!
- Take photos of the piles of index cards.
- You'll revisit the content in other exercises. Save it for now.

Later

- It isn't a bad idea to test some of the priorities with a paid campaign or a sales pitch. However, this information may change again as you proceed. So, experiment lightly.

Exercise 1.2: Templates and Examples

- **Figure 4:** Example of "What Is It?" for an Online Store for Pet Supply, Training, and Certification Needed for Working Service Dogs with the Bold Text Showing Purpose-aligned Content
- **Figure 5:** Working Dogs Company Purpose

Figure 4: Example of "What Is It?" for an Online Store for Pet Supply, Training, and Certification Needed for Working Service Dogs with the Bold Text Showing Purpose-aligned Content

Features pulled from marketing materials	Training	Quality Treats	Harness/Vests IDs	Toys & Supplies	Working Dog Qualification	Certification	Registration	Is this important?
Priority 1	*Get professional **(certified)** Emotional Support Animal Training	Clicker training (**reward-motivation**) treats	*Fast (**timely**) access to photo **IDs/certification (digital)**	Clicker	Qualifying conditions (physical and mental health diagnosis)	*Trusted certification (**authentic**)	***Official requirements for service animal status**	Improve travel experience
Priority 2	***Convenient online training** is as effective as in-person (and less expensive)	Healthy (**natural ingredients**)	*Official harness with handle (**service animal**)	Treat bags	***Medical diagnosis documents** (Doctors' letters)	*Qualifying conditions (physical and mental health diagnosis)	***Trusted** as of U.S. Service and Support Animal Registration Database (**only source or compliance**)	*(Help if rights are violated)
Priority 3	***Trusted training** (not scam/ fraudulent sites)	Organic vegetable (meat-free) snacks	*Dog packs (**medical supply packs**)	Leashes	***Understand** Therapy dog vs **Service dog requirements**	**Less expensive than in-person**	***Process for legal assistance**	
			Patches (people and dog)			Activities dogs need to perform	*(Free) **access to National Database** (compliance?)	

Figure 4 also shows an asterisk (*) if the content is a priority **AND** it matches the brand's purpose. This indicates potential key differentiators that either alone or in combination, are a unique offering.

Figure 5: Working Dogs Company Purpose

Working Dog's Company Purpose

Committed to individuals, handlers, pet parents and their working dogs who need a single, trusted resource and registry to instantly verify, identify, and help understand and enforce the legal rights of people and animals covered by the Americans with Disability Act. Provide training and support to increase the number of emotional support and service dogs by offering affordable online training and resources.

The Client Story

Do You Have a New Product or Is It a Dramatic Pivot Point for Your Brand?

Innovation can be a tricky thing. As an organization, you must respond to customer requests and remain committed to improving the brand experience. Sometimes innovation leads to a new product or service that could be a game-changer. The new product or service can start with a small client request – a one-off or a temporary Band Aid solution. It is often well received – so much so that it may ignite internal momentum to make it a more extensive offering. Or it might even be a catalyst for a change in direction. But is it?

I once had a technology firm in the business intelligence workflow space. We realized that lots of communication happened outside the established workflow process. The emails, chats, meetings, and conversations drove decisions but often sat outside the corporate-designed workflow system. It's a problem if you are in the business intelligence technology space but aren't capturing the intelligence outside your system. It was particularly problematic when it came to fast-paced, complex decisions like closing sales.

The client created a small prototype that could dynamically capture conversations and decisions for workflows that did not have an established process and weren't in their installed system. The development of the prototype ignited an existential crisis. To support internal workflow, employees need a way to communicate and collaborate on what they need to do and who they need to do it with. The prototype exposed the fact that the multi-million-dollar application was not capturing the dynamic intelligence of the collaborations and discussions outside the established workflow – in chats, emails, calls, conversations, meetings, and messages. The prototype thus became a strategy dilemma. What is it that business intelligence customers need? Is it a *different* system that captures dynamic workflow? Is it a product to improve the existing business intelligence workflow? Was the prototype an excellent idea? Yes. One that clients would use? Well, that was not so clear.

The engineering team built a prototype, and existing customers tested it. Two common problems became evident. First, the customer interviews after they tried the prototype did not provide an explicit go/no-go direction. Second, the prototype did not include a specific use case to verify feature selection. The company was stuck in the prototype stage, with unclear features and messaging. So, we had to help the team determine **what is it** that they had exactly.

During the "What Is It?" session, a fundamental problem emerged. The potential new product sat in the busy, confusing collaboration space. The desire to capture the dynamic workflow of internal processes that lay outside the system could be described either in terms of "transparency" or "Big Brother". Identifying and prioritizing the features became a battle between the product development and the marketing teams. In the simple workshop, we uncovered the fact that the product itself would have to acknowledge that customers weren't currently using the business intelligence workflow system the company sold. It was tricky to offer something so radical. It wasn't just a new product line. It was a new direction.

During the workshop, deep conversations brought to the surface the fragility of introducing a new product that highlighted the current technology's flaws. While the engineering team wanted to prioritize features like dynamic collaboration across the enterprise, the marketing team was more interested in features that could capture a workflow process where none had previously existed. After two years of development, this was a long overdue session, which helped them understand the new technology's impact on the product strategy.

The grid template allowed engineering and marketing to define how they should move forward. They had to either clarify what the product needed to be to augment the existing technology or investigate the possibility that the new product could be the brand's future. Sometimes, asking "What is it?" opens a massive can of worms. Sticking with the workshops and frameworks will allow you to make critical decisions.

The weeks of working through all the messaging strategy workshops, customer interviews, industry research, customer identification, and funding discussions culminated with a final meeting with the CEO. He asked a simple question. Could this new product be the future of his company? The answer was clear. No! The messaging workshop exercises revealed a considerable risk; it was a product that would cannibalize the existing business. And it was one that customers didn't want because they wanted the freedom to collaborate freely in the methods that made sense for them at the time. No amount of messaging was going to create demand. Sometimes, the answer may not be what your team wanted, but it can still save your brand from disastrous distractions and get you to buckle down on precisely what your customers love about you.

Chapter 2

Who Is Experiencing the Pain?

Key Idea

A brand needs to identify customers who will value its products and services. When asked who can benefit from your brand, the accepted response is to answer with a role. Identifying customers by their position is an ingrained method of marketing segmentation and targeting. Perhaps it is based on the days when marketing and sales systems depended on direct, face-to-face selling. A direct sales force did a great deal of cold calling on businesses – just walking into the office and asking to speak with someone who holds a particular role. Back then, if you sold copy paper, you were clearly in the office supplies space and targeting office managers. Asking to talk to the person who filled a role was the first step in building a customer base and relationship. There's a reason there are still "no soliciting signs" – it was an intrusive method that frustrated everyone.

The role-first approach was always a shortcut fraught with failure. Right out of the gate, it ignores the foundational principles of a customer-centric approach. Latching onto role-based marketing assumes that all people with a role are the same: they have the exact needs and thus are equally qualified to be your customer. Then you experience this failure in ways we are all used to in business today: unqualified leads, long, drawn-out closing cycles, and prospects who ghost you, because they don't believe they need your product or service.

Suppose your ideal customer is a Chief Technology Officer (CTO). In that case, your messaging, campaigns, sales tools, onboarding process, and products will be focused on all or most Chief Technology Officers. There may be some segmentation, for example, you might focus on Chief Technology Officers in healthcare or finance industries. However, the point is that your potential customer pool is everyone who has a particular role in that industry. Attempts to dig deeper into the potential customer, such as understanding the issues Chief Technology Officers face or identifying specific attributes, are also rooted in the role. Brands may add circumstantial evidence to narrow down prospective customers. For instance, you might target Chief Technology Officers in financing looking for a solution to support remote workers. Well, that is still a wide swath of people with very little in common.

Pursuing the roles is so embedded in our marketing approach that we sometimes don't stop even when it fails. When the CTOs keep telling you they don't need your products and services, you continue to target them because they are considered decision-makers. Confronted with evidence that the person desperate for a solution is a lower-level title, brands remain fixated on the person in a role who has no emotional connection to the problem they claim they can resolve. In the business-to-business and business-to-consumer model, if the target customer is defined as a role and not a person, you won't be able to adopt a customer-centric approach.

You will market and sell to the roles (CEO, CTO, CFO) or groups (salespeople, analysts, finance people, project managers). In the business-to-consumer model, you often end up marketing and selling to roles (moms, dads, decision-makers) or groups (teachers, shoppers, retirees).

Are all CTOs the same? Is your version of what a CTO is different from mine? The answer is yes. When you remain role-centric, you avoid knowing the person behind the role. You don't develop a profound understanding and agreement on who the CTO actually is. What are they facing? How do they feel about the constraints they face? What does it feel like to be in their role right now and in this market?

What Is Wrong with Current Methods?

Embracing a customer-centric approach does not mean giving up marketing and selling to the highest-ranking role. However, it does mean examining the specific situations and people involved in the problem you are trying to address. A single role does not own a problem. Many roles experience problems – and finding the positions connected to the problem is far more valuable for your brand.

To pivot away from targeting a single primary role involves a simple change from asking, "Who is the decision-maker?" to asking, "Who is experiencing the pain?" If the decision-maker is not directly experiencing the pain, it will never be a priority for them. You will therefore be stuck spending a great deal of time, money, and effort educating the decision-maker about a problem they don't feel. That is an unproductive and ineffective cycle. When you let go of asking, "Who is my decision maker?" and ask, 'Who is experiencing the pain?" you are forced to look anew at those who are frustrated with their current situation. You must look again for the people you may have ignored. The question "Who is experiencing the pain?" gives you the freedom to see the problem from the viewpoint of ALL the potential customers experiencing it. The customers with a strong emotional need to make the pain disappear are the ones you want to focus on.

Think of this shift as a chance to reset – a customer insight exercise designed to understand the people, their roles, and their emotional responses to the problem you can solve. You can probe into the way the people who experience this issue interact with frustrating processes, rules, and systems. You want to identify the way they share this frustration. A vital aspect of the customer-centric approach is determining how many people and roles within a given industry, department, or situation experience the pain. You are looking for scenarios where more than one person is experiencing a strong negative emotion and can point to measurable inefficiencies.

Revisiting the roles you target and committing to a deeper understanding of the problem from the perspective of all roles will unlock a more robust messaging strategy for what will likely be a better market fit. Asking the question, "Who is experiencing the pain?" may reveal a very different industry, department, and process. It will probably help you to identify a series of decision-makers who have the power and the inclination to make things better. It will help you to map the process, circumstances, and ecosystem where you add value.

When Do You Need to Address This?

You know you need this when your prospects do not recognize that they have a problem you can solve or do not believe it is a priority. They may also ask how you are different from the systems they already have in place. Or, worse, getting close to a potential sale is impossible because your audience simply doesn't think they need you. Some tell-tale signs you may be experiencing are:

Poor Lead Generation

Focusing on roles results in generic messaging that doesn't appeal to anyone. It is a broad, ineffective approach because it encompasses your version of the role and its problems from YOUR perspective.

Stalled Sales Presentations

The most challenging situation is when you're halfway into the sales presentation, and both you and the prospects realize they don't have the problems you said they have. They may tell you they are the wrong person to talk to or, worse, that the problem doesn't exist in their organization. This can be uncomfortable and sets up an even steeper hill to climb.

Unsubscribes

A significant indicator that you are too focused on the roles is the number of unsubscribes you get – especially early in the onboarding process. Those initial few messages are delicate and concentrated on moving a prospect along a path built on trust. If there is a significant level of unsubscribes, it is a sure sign that you are your own obstacle.

Why Doing This Now Will Get You a Better ROI

Targeting a single decision-maker with a high-level role is a shortcut that often gets you lost. Do you know many CEOs who create a business case? The CFO signs off on decisions but doesn't make them. Focusing on a single role and title is meaningless. You need to look deeper at the problems you can solve and who has the power and responsibility to fix them. Who owns the problem? Who within the organization is the valid user, and who is the actual decision-maker?

This may sound a bit like account-based selling, but the difference here is to look at the ecosystem – find who is experiencing the pain and be open to the fact that the role(s) may differ from one company to the other. And two people in the same role in similar companies can experience the pain differently. If, after this exercise, you agree that it's the CEO, you need to decide on the type of person behind the role. Then you need to refine the answer from "All CEOs" to "Specific CEOs." Specifics matter. Specifics about the problems and obstacles the person is facing – from their perspective. How do they view their strengths and weaknesses? How do they see the world? Not doing this exercise will lead to a great deal of wasted time and disappointment.

With the mounting pressure to deliver big wins, the instinct is to keep swinging for a home run. If you want to derive an ROI from this exercise, think about the alternative. What would happen if you launched an extensive campaign, increased paid advertising, or cast a wider net without refining your idea of your target customer? In that case, all those will lead to the same result: wasted dollars convincing people who don't have a problem that they do. What's that costing you?

In the construct of business, we believe we know what customers will value. We have no doubt that the products and services we provide will solve their problem. However, somewhere along the way, you mixed up "Thinking LIKE the customer" with "Thinking OF the customer". When you think like a customer, you miss out on seeing how their role in their work-life affects other positions. Those roles are secondary relationships. When you create value for a single position, like a physician, how does it affect patients, nurses, families, specialists, lab technicians, and home healthcare?

Value creation has a ripple effect – but you still need to throw the stone in the right pond.

How to Fix It - Workshop and Exercises

Who Is Experiencing The Pain?

This workshop helps you see your customer's ecosystem – to observe the dynamics of their lives that relate to the solution you provide.

As much as possible, this step is about looking anew at the people you are targeting. What are the issues and problems they face WITH one another? Where are the gaps in their understanding and thinking? How are their environment, culture, and regulations preventing them from excelling? What are their key performance indicators? What behaviors are routine? Where are they stuck? Who is involved in the status quo?

This is a two-part exercise. The first exercise focuses on the question of who is experiencing the pain. It is not about targeting a single role but drafting the ecosystem around it. No role is an island. We dig deeper into the people and their functions in the second exercise. Think of people at work as mini-networks. Look for the ways the roles connect with others. Consider the processes, information exchange, relationship value, and shared collective vital indicators. You are trying to find the connections within the ecosystem where you offer the most value.

Exercise 2.1: The Role Matrix

Timeframe
45 minutes

Focus
Information Sharing | Problem-solving Ideation

Participant Instructions
This is a card sorting exercise in which each participant will identify the front-line people experiencing pain due to NOT having your solution. It is NOT about identifying the ultimate decision-maker. Your task is to recognize the roles involved in identifying, evaluating, purchasing, and implementing the solution. The roles you propose must have a direct connection to other roles. Since this is a reset, you are encouraged to re-introduce roles that have previously been sidelined because they were not considered decision-makers. If possible, bring to light those you know could benefit greatly but who have not been a focus.

Facilitator Instructions
This ideation session permits you and the team to determine who is experiencing the problem. Part of this exercise is to find a single scenario, industry, and situation that intensely experiences pain. Re-introduce roles previously dismissed as "not decision-makers" and add positions that experience the problem – even if they experience it as an extension of someone else's role. Seek the value exchange for every role.

You'll need index cards or post-it notes for each participant. If you are using index cards, you may choose to provide pre-printed index cards with the roles you know will be mentioned. However, blank index cards should also be available to allow participants to add new roles.

Step-by-Step Guideline

The pace and timeframe may be shorter or longer. Use the suggestions below as a guide and, if necessary, break them into smaller sessions.

10 minutes

1. Ask participants to list a role for each person experiencing the pain your product/solution solves. This is not about identifying the role of the ultimate decision-maker, but all the people directly affected. Identifying new roles is good. You can even provide prompts to participants to think outside the box. "What about roles from different industries?" or "Think about people who often contact us, but we did not pursue them" Nothing should be off the table. As the participants do this, outline the Role Matrix (see Figure 6) on the board.

5 minutes

2. Ask participants to prioritize the cards by the role of the people who are experiencing the pain the most. Remind them to think of scenarios in which the person in that role would need a better solution.

15 minutes

3. One person will begin to recite their belief for who is the highest priority. As they do, you can start to add the role to the Role Matrix.
    - Begin to reorganize roles on a role matrix
    - Each row should relate to a specific industry
        - When you can, place the role on the matrix in the order your participant believes is highest priority to lowest priority.
        - Don't worry about getting the primary and secondary roles in order. That will be part of the next exercise.

- As participants share their ideas, a few exciting connections will occur.
    - Many might mention the same roles but have them in a different order of pain level. Acknowledge this and allow discussion with these "almost connections".
    - When roles that seem to be a small market are identified, you or the participants may believe the market is tiny. However, keep these in the matrix for now.

4. As you add roles in an industry, you are looking for roles that share or experience pain.
    - Discuss the context of related roles. For example, is an Emergency Room Doctor different from a Primary Care Doctor, or do they both experience the same, related problem?

15 minutes

5. Ask participants to identify any additional roles, or consolidate roles that are probably the same. In this step, the participants may discuss cases where the experience of two positions (the emergency room doctor vs. a primary care doctor) is the same and when it might be different.
6. If this exercise gets heated, that is good! Use your best judgment to consolidate or not. You might need to revisit as the use/business case develops.

What To Do Next

Now

- Photograph the whiteboard or save the PowerPoint. This initial example will be reworked in other ways, so you'll need to capture this version.
- In addition, you may need to revisit another industry, which will give you a great starting point.

Later

- You'll use this grid to create prioritized audiences across multiple industries. The primary prioritized audiences (column 1) should have similarities in terms of their role's importance and primary function. For instance, in Figure 8, nurses, teachers, and mortgage loan officers deal with many people daily, handle confidential information, and are governed by a compliance standard.

Exercise 2.1: Templates and Examples

- **Figure 6:** Exercise 2.1 Role Matrix
- **Figure 7:** Exercise 2.1 Role Matrix Template
- **Figure 8:** Example of Exercise 2.1 Role Matrix (Not Prioritized)
- **Figure 9:** Example of Exercise 2.1 Role Matrix for Technology Firm Prioritized by Industry and Role

Figure 6: Exercise 2.1 Role Matrix

Industry A	Important Role to You	Important Role to You	Important Role to You	Important Role to You
Industry B	Important Role to You	Important Role to You	Important Role to You	Important Role to You
Industry C	Important Role to You	Important Role to You	Important Role to You	Important Role to You

Figure 6: You are capturing industries that are important to your business and the direct and indirect roles your products and services impact. The roles should include all the people who will interact with your products or services and those who will benefit from others' interactions. Add the industry in the first column and the roles related to that industry will be added to the row.

Figure 7: Exercise 2.1 Role Matrix Template

Industry A	Primary Role A	Secondary Role A-1	Secondary Role A-2	Secondary Role A-3	Secondary Role A-4
Industry B	Primary Role B	Secondary Role B-1	Secondary Role B-2	Secondary Role B-3	Secondary Role B-4
Industry C	Primary Role C	Secondary Role C-1	Secondary Role C-2	Secondary Role C-3	Secondary Role C-4

In **Figure 7**, there is a great deal of moving the roles around and subdividing the industry. Use the grid to organize roles and industries along a row. Your task is to identify the primary role. The order of the secondary roles doesn't matter much at this point. You'll continue to work on this in other exercises.

Figure 8: Example of Exercise 2.1 Role Matrix (not prioritized)

Industry A	Nurses	Lab Techs	Physicians	Patients	Patient Advocate
Industry B	Teachers	Coach	Students	Guidance Counselors	Classroom Aides
Industry C	Mortgage Loan Officer	Person Buying Home	Loan Underwriter	Home Inspector	Real Estate Agent

Figure 8 shows that the industries can be high-level – Healthcare, Education, and Finance, or, if you know the specific subcategories, you can select those instead (e.g. Healthcare facilities is a subindustry and could include clinics, pharmacies, labs, hospitals) The above figure is an example of the content in an initial session. The roles and industries aren't prioritized yet.

Figure 9: Example of Exercise 2.1 Role Matrix for Technology Firm Prioritized by Industry and Role

		Primary	Secondary	Secondary 2	Secondary 3	Secondary 4	Secondary 5	Secondary 6
Industry A	Healthcare	**Physicians**	Patients	patients	Patient advocate	Radiologists / specialists	Visiting nurses/home health care	Health information manager
Industry B	Education	**Students**	Teachers	Guidance counselors	Classroom aides	Guidance counselors	Parents	Parent-Teacher
Industry C	Real estate	**Buyer**	Seller	Home inspector	Real estate agent	House Inspector	Banker / Mortgage Lender	

Figure 9: In this example of the industries that require the sharing of confidential documents, we can see how many roles and relationships there are. Understanding the primary roles and the relationships allows for a customer-centric understanding of the environment in which your customers live. And the primary customers, at this point, still need to be tested.

This matrix serves two functions. It helps you see which industry, prioritized roles, and more significant relationships you need to penetrate. In the example above, the client wanted to go after healthcare, legal, and government simultaneously, and with a limited budget. Whenever the marketing team launched a campaign, someone in the organization would proclaim it was aimed in the wrong direction. This pattern kept repeating with no progress.

Highlight the rich roles and the number of interactions between the roles. This matrix demonstrates that people in multiple roles may need the product or service and consider it valuable. The primary role of "Physicians" is not specific enough. We need to know what kind of Physician. Will it be a Surgeon, Primary Care, Emergency Room, or Specialist? While the participants may think the Physician is the appropriate target, other roles are more substantial.

You can imagine there is a big disconnect between physicians, students, and buyers. Within their respective roles, these are very different types of people who manage very different types of relationships with the ecosystem they are currently in. This will create a problem if you think you can market the same product or service across multiple industries. Each role (physician, student, and buyer) would need entirely different messaging. And yet, we often look at our customers as having the same pain and needing the same solution.

Exercise 2.2: What Will Each Role Value?

Timeframe

20 minutes

Focus

Collaborative Creation | Design Thinking

Participant Instructions

Value creation is an exchange. It is not a negotiation. It is not a compromise. And it is not one-dimensional. This exercise reveals the multi-dimensional value exchanged between various roles. Focus only on the one industry that you think is your strongest.

Facilitator Instructions

In this exercise, expect a little bit of mess. The group will be trying to articulate two things: the scenario that best fits the solution AND who the primary role is. Two scenarios may work: be ready to keep them separate.

Step-by-Step Guideline

Salient bias can creep into this exercise. Watch out for thinking based on the last deal won or lost. Look for examples of how your customers run their business, not examples of how you think it should run.

10 Minutes

1. Stay focused on a single industry.

2. Ask participants to discuss scenarios involving primary and secondary users.
    - Participants should not be allowed to squelch ideas during this stage. Collaborate on a typical, relatable scenario.

5 Minutes

3. Home in on one scenario and identify the value exchange between the primary and secondary users. You can do this in one of two ways:
    - You can have participants write the values on post-it that you will then transfer to the whiteboard, or you can facilitate a whiteboard session

10 minutes

4. There can be many nuances when it comes to the value. As you continue this discussion, probe these nuances. If the participant provides value from the brand's perspective, probing questions can shift the focus to the value from customer's viewpoint.
    - Look for the values the customers want.

What To Do Next

Now

- Photograph the whiteboard as it is!
- Capture the values. If the participant used post-its, be sure to photograph them, too.
- Highlight the values and connections the customers want.

Later

- Continue with Chapter 3.

Exercise 2.2: Templates and Examples

- **Figure 10:** Template for Exercise 2.2: Value Exchange Ecosystem™ between Roles
- **Figure 11a:** Example of The Value Exchange Ecosystem™ for Healthcare
- **Figure 11b:** Example of Value Exchange Ecosystem between Roles in a Healthcare Situation for Sharing Documents with Participant's Notes
- **Figure 11c:** Example of Which Role Receives the MOST Value in this Exchange

Figure 10: Template for Exercise 2.2 Value Exchange Ecosystem™ between Roles

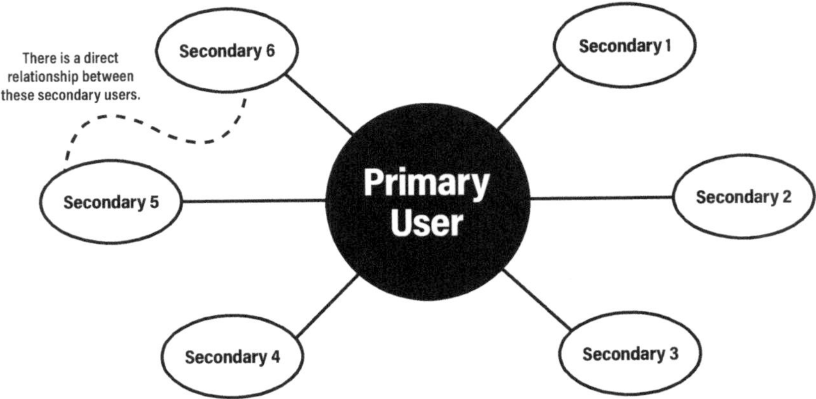

In **figure 10**, you are trying to verify who the primary user is. This structure will help you identify the primary and secondary customers. It serves as a framework to visualize users and their relationships with one another and with your product/service. The primary user may change as you add content to this diagram. The order of the secondary users may also shift. You can use dotted lines to show relationships between secondary users. As you continue using this structure, you may find that the primary user is not who you initially expected. And that can be a powerful revelation.

Figure 11a: Example of The Value Exchange Ecosystem™ for Healthcare

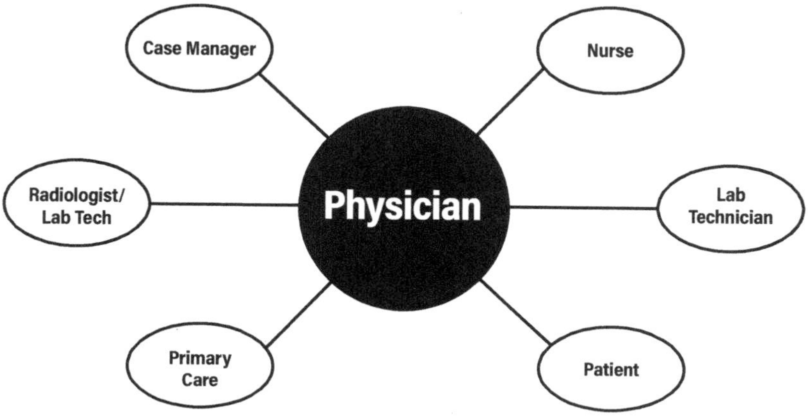

This figure shows the preliminary identification of product users. The physician is considered the person with the most power to make decisions. As we progress, this MAY change.

Figure 11b: Example of Value Exchange Ecosystem™ between Roles in a Healthcare Situation for Sharing Documents with Participant's Notes

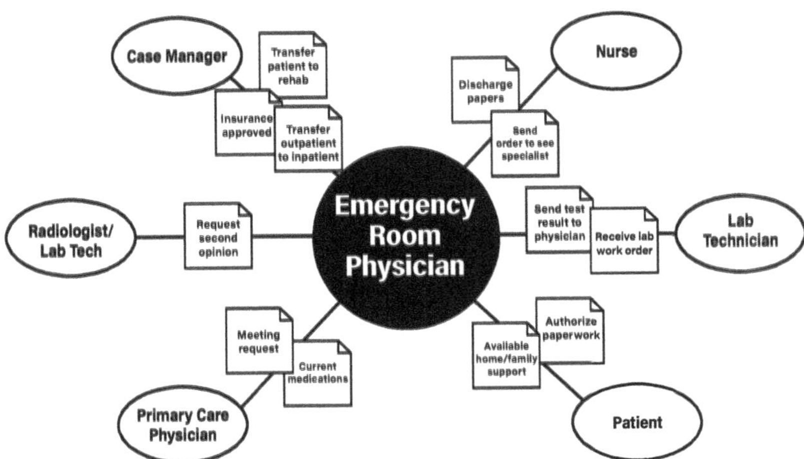

Here we see a session where participants listed the activities related to the experience of sharing private information within a hospital emergency room. The post-its include situations where confidential information must be shared. Here the Emergency Room Physician is still the primary target audience. However, the patient is the hospital's customer, and all information requested and exchanged is related to the patient.

Figure 11c: Which Role Receives the MOST Value in this Exchange

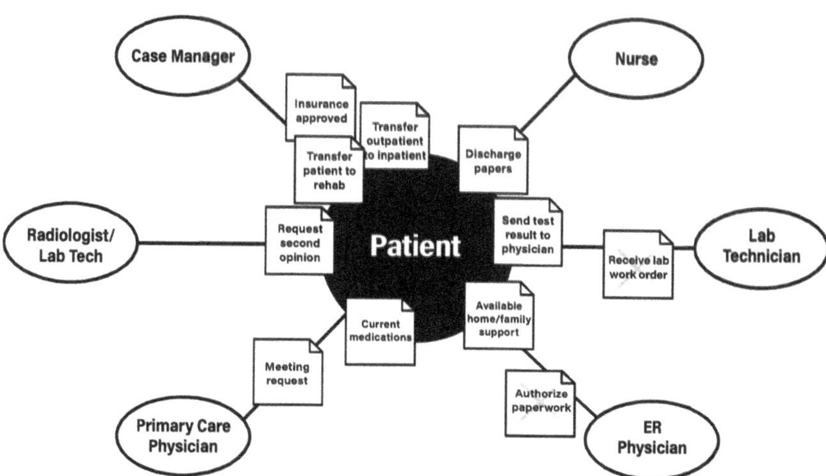

A slightly different view is created by the question of who receives the MOST value in the ecosystem. Ultimately, the patient is the center of all exchanges. They are the key person in the ecosystem and gain the most value. The post-it examples marked with an X are items the patient doesn't see or experience. The emergency room doctor might initially be perceived as the primary role for confidential information technology, but the patient is the role who would gain the most benefit. This changes the messaging and positioning ultimately. It is for and about the patient.

The Client Story

Is the Best Buyer Always the One in the Most Pain?

There is always some resistance to the idea of accepting a new primary customer. This may be related to prestige – by that, I mean brands like to pick the most influential and reputable buyer. Or participants may have a belief that the work they have already been investing in needs more time. Focusing on the wrong primary customer and a lack of understanding of the value ecosystem will put you on a direct path to slow growth.

I once worked with a publishing client in the college education space. They had a new textbook built on rich, highly engaging classroom experiences students loved. It was a book designed to help professors learn how to teach with the level of excitement and energy students crave. The content was viral. Students could share it online. The concepts used movies, music, news, and pop culture to explain economic concepts.

The difficulty of selling new textbooks is that it requires rebuilding the course. Once a book was part of a course, a professor didn't often make drastic changes. For the publisher, this means long-lasting, continuous revenue once a textbook is adopted. Conversely, getting professors to consider a new book is a complex task. The act of adding a new textbook requires the professors to do much work to redesign the course and change the assignments, homework, and classroom lectures.

Figure 12a: Roles within College Course Textbook Selection

Full-Time Professor	Course Section Leader	Department Chair	Adjunct/ Part-Time Lecturer	Student	Teaching Assistant	Publisher

Looking at the college education value ecosystem, you find varying roles and relationships: Publishers, Professors, Course Section Leaders, Department Chairs, Adjunct Lecturers, Teaching Assistants, and Students.

We knew that full-time professors were challenging to convince. They required a long sales cycle, and no other role seemed viable as a target. Interviews showed that students could use online resources to find help with homework. So, the longer a professor used the same textbook and curriculum, the more likely the students would be able to see the materials, answers, and examples from previous students' work online. Also, students were becoming more vocal about how they wanted to engage in the classroom. There was a high demand for relevant material – more project-based learning and real-world connections. Universities began to listen closely to how students wanted to learn and become more aware of the costs associated with textbooks and resources needed for classroom instruction.

If you look at the value of the full-time professor as the primary target, there isn't anything of value. There is no incentive to change textbooks. In addition, it would take years to convert a professor to adopt a new book.

Figure 12b: Value Exchange Ecosystem™ between Roles in Selecting College Course Textbook

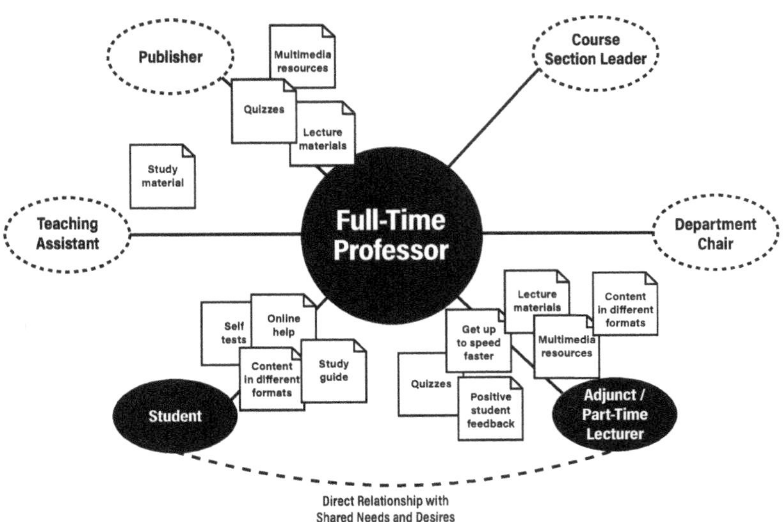

Figure 12b shows the students' and adjunct professors' needs and desires are tightly related.

The adjunct sometimes needs to develop a course quickly and have a positive classroom experience the first time to continue working at the college or university. When selecting a textbook, an adjunct who wants to create a great course would likely choose a textbook with all the features students love. Ultimately, the students are central to the educational system.

Figure 12c: Adjunct Professor and Students Match the Publisher's Needs and Desire

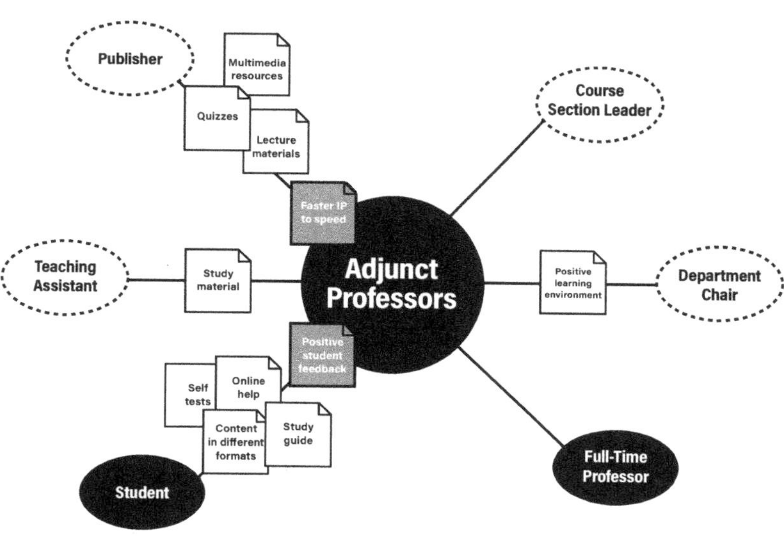

Figure 12b shows the students' and adjunct professors' needs and desires are tightly related.

If you look closely at the adjunct / part-time lecturer, several factors are shared between an adjunct professor and students. They do not have an existing textbook. They need to get up to speed quickly – create a course from scratch in a relatively short period. They need to create a positive experience right away. Adjunct professors would be an excellent target for a new textbook – especially one with proven rich content to help students learn concepts and enable rich engagement.

The publisher shifted the focus to part-time economic lecturers who needed current material students loved. The secondary audience became the students who were allowed to rate and share content online. Students brought the new textbook exercises, lecture materials, and classroom examples into their classrooms and to the attention of full-time professors. In short order, full-time professors and teaching assistants finding their students using another textbook's materials were promoted to adopt the new textbook.

It was a novel approach that worked. The shift to a slightly different audience allowed the publisher to close sales sooner and expand more rapidly by building a pull strategy from students. This audience had become more potent in their ability to influence the way they learned.

Chapter 3

What Do Customers Want?

Key Idea

When developing products and services, you generally perform competitive analysis. For founders with significant experience, competitive research may require a few hours scouring websites and other sources seeking product details that guide the creation of their product offering. Or it might take a more in-depth market evaluation, including customer interviews, product testing, and market research, to understand what is absent from the market today. In designing a more robust alternative, you look for scenarios where your products and services will be considered a more valuable offering. Competitive product evaluation is supposed to be an evidence-based, unbiased exercise. It makes sense to study the existing products and services to guide the design of your products and services. However, focusing on the features and benefits of existing market offerings can keep brands from seeing customers' wants and needs.

If you were designing a better No. 2 yellow pencil, you might want to focus on small changes to existing features—like the lead so it doesn't break easily or alter the eraser so it doesn't leave those annoying crumbs you need to brush off the paper. If you were the founder of a *new* writing instruments company, you are looking for ways to differentiate your alternative to pencils. When you consider your new alternative to the traditional No. 2 pencil, your mind focuses on the features and benefits. Since you must build a better pencil and your engineering team needs specifications and functional requirements, this seems the logical approach. The same is true for service-based businesses. If you were the founder of an accounting firm, you might study the competition to see if they are project-based or put on retainer. Do they specialize in non-profit or tax preparation? Are they fully remote, or do they come to your office weekly? And what does that mean for how you will position your firm?

In the product development process, you are focused on creating products that people will want based on features and benefits that are currently available and your strength and skillsets. Compiling a comparison feature set is simple when it comes to being asked what makes you better. Point to a web page or product sheet with all the checkmarks that show what you have that competitors do not. "Look at this list of what we provide! See how we are better!" This is straightforward. But it is a trap. The product/service development feature/benefits process directly influences the sales process – it becomes a continuation of the feature/benefit messaging based on the assumption that you understand the needs and wants of the customer. By doing thorough research, you could evaluate what your prospective customers need and want unbiasedly – but this rarely happens.

In the initial quest to bring a different product or service to market, founding teams often ignore the far more powerful and profitable issue – what your customers want and need. The blinders of product development prevent them from seeing the environment from the viewpoint of the prospective customer. During the initial investigation, data or responses that didn't match the feature or benefit were cast aside. And once they are on the path of feature and benefit-rich argument, the idea that perhaps the customers don't want those features is met with significant resistance.

Academic scholars use the concept of value exchange to describe the transactional relationship between a consumer and a brand. Conceptually, you understand it is an "exchange of value". However, the word "value" can easily slip into the features-first mindset. If I ask a marketer who sells hammers, "what does your customer value?" they may respond, "An affordable hammer that is not too heavy and that fits nicely in their hand". If I have a conversation with a potential customer about what they need, I might hear they need to feel comfortable making home improvements to save money for their kid's college. Potential customers who want to embark on home improvements as part of a plan to save money for their kids will spend more on a quality hammer, as they need to reach their goal.

Buying is need-based. A person's inner needs and wants – be it fear, insecurity, boredom, emotional pain, or unfilled wishes – are what drive purchases. You need to be careful that needs do not become secondary to features. Swap out the idea of value for the need to keep from slipping to a focus on features. Yes, business is about creating value. Creating value is the exchange of products and services. The exchange of products and services represents the fulfillment of the brand promise – and your promise to satisfy the wants or needs of your customers.

If I am doing work on my house, you may think I am buying a hammer to nail things. When I buy a hammer, I want features – for instance, the handle must feel right in my hands, while the weight needs to match my swing and become an extension of me. I am buying a hammer to build things. But deeper down, I want to feel capable of fixing a problem. I want to experience a sense of pride and accomplishment.

What Is Wrong with Current Methods?

When trying to understand an audience's wants and needs, it feels safer to stay on the surface – to keep a business mindset that does not look at the person holistically. It takes time and concerted effort to dig deeper into what potential customers want. There is often pressure and resistance within organizations that genuinely believe they "know their customer." Considering the customer's perspective – looking deeply at their experiences, circumstances, situations, and scenarios where you could help – may feel like it will upend the brand. And you may feel that it is not needed, or that it is not the right time for it.

In addition to market research, the marketing and product teams might use buyer personas, empathy maps, and customer journeys to home in on the target market. Marketers are looking for who will be the best match for these features and benefits. Buyer personas, empathy maps, and customer journey diagrams are excellent tools when the content and data are unbiased. However, when marketers are constrained at a high level, formulaic demographic, psychographic, and consumer insights that confirm the existing brand beliefs are at risk of failing. Instead of listening to consumer needs, marketers tend to search for a market.

The buyer personas, empathy map, and customer journeys help product and service design. But if these market tools are produced after you have built the products and services, it creates a backward engineering scenario. You can't hear what customers want and need when looking for comments and intentions that support the existing features and benefits. If your products and services are only slightly different from competitors, it doesn't help your sales team tell a compelling story. Competitors will rapidly alter their features and benefits to counter your brand. You'll be in a highly competitive market when you could have been in a market of one – a brand or provider that radically understands the wants and needs of their customers.

When Do You Need to Address This?

You know you need this when you can't see the difference between you and your competitors. Or you might need this if you and your sales team struggle during a demonstration that quickly devolves into a feature/benefit comparison with lots of conversation about discount pricing because the value discussion is ignored or not believed. This might feel like every sale is an uphill battle fighting objection after objection.

Unproductive Demonstrations

You're five minutes into the pitch, and your prospective customer begins to ask questions that quickly go into a significant comparison with your competitor, ultimately taking the entire presentation off the rails.

Stalled Sales / Fewer Closing

After you demonstrate your features and benefits, prospects or existing customers discuss how they do it differently at their company. This can be seen as a form of frustration where you may think the customer/prospect is asking for customization or struggling with the question, "Is this a good fit?"

Requesting Discount Conversations

If you notice an increase in customers asking for discounts either early or late in the process, this may indicate that they believe they are making a compromise on selecting you. This indicates that they aren't getting what they want or need.

Why Doing This Now Will Get You a Better ROI

Deep customer insight takes time and good listening – attributes that many of us lack. The need for fast results gets in the way of excellent results. If you can do something that changes an industry or disrupts a market, it will make competitors irrelevant and catapult you ahead. Addiction to immediacy focuses us on short-term objectives – make a simple website, get fast (but not qualified) leads, and let's create a scattershot approach to advertising and call it brand awareness. Awareness of what? It gets you thinking; why are brands rushing to get nowhere fast? Is it the thousands of dollars for deep customer insight and a few months conducting research you need to avoid or the possibility that what you developed isn't something customers need? Knowing your customers intimately means you are sure of what they want. You can then produce what they need, and they will trust you when you say you can provide it. The alternative is to struggle daily to build an ROI story in click-through rates, fuzzy engagement measurements, and incremental sales that don't scale.

The digital experience is your differentiator. You must know the customer better than anyone else. The experience of your site, trial offer, onboarding, customer support, training, upgrades, and consumption requires relationship building. Fear the quick and easy. Strive for simplicity. But bear in mind that simple takes enormous hard work. Simple is being there at the right time with the right solution for the right person. To accomplish simple things, spend the time and money on knowing what customers want.

How to Fix It - Workshop and Exercises

What Do They Need?

Previously you looked at the customer and their world. Now, you look at *how* the customer is feeling in their ecosystem. Here we want to know the customer's emotional state to identify who might be ready to adopt a new product or service. In the first exercise, you'll focus on how their environment, beliefs, and culture affect their readiness to make a change. Be ready for elevated discussions with a few participants intensely debating the issues. Allow productive discussions to play out if they move the idea forward.

In the second exercise, you'll get a closer look at the reality of your brand promise by exploring the emotional shift you can offer and the likelihood that your customers will work with you to purchase, adopt, use, and champion your brand. Consider this exercise a reality check. You may believe your customers want efficiency when they want to stop feeling trapped in the way of doing things that no longer make sense. You can imagine that an efficient message might not do very well when the person you sell to feels they can't escape the current situation.

In the third exercise, we introduce the emotional wheel. If, for instance, a customer is looking for a solution because they are feeling fear in their ability to do their job, it is crucial to understand how the fear is manifesting. Are they afraid, anxious, worried, or overwhelmed? If your customer is worried, you might say, "Don't worry, I've done this before, and it will be alright. Your message would be reassuring. If your audience is overwhelmed, you might need to approach it from an angle that says, "Let's break this down into smaller steps. Here is one thing you can do right now." That way, you'd provide a soothing, encouraging tone. Knowing which tone to take allows you to see the path they want to take to feel something different. When in pain, the customer wants relief. If you aren't emotionally aligned with them, you can't use the best words, tone, message, creativity, and approach to help them travel across the emotional wheel to feel something different.

♥ **Note:** *The Emotional Wheel is an adaptation of Mike Bostock's adaptation of Geoffrey Roberts' Emotion Wheel using D3's partition layout. Robert's 2015 work appears to be based on a vocabulary wheel by Kaitlin Robbs from 2014, which in turn seems to be based on The Feeling Wheel published by Gloria Willcox in 1982.*

Exercise 3.1: What Is The Need?

Timeframe

75 minutes

Focus

Consumer Insight | Empathy

Participant Instructions

This is a multi-step exercise designed to help you filter the roles you could serve by getting more insight into the human experience within the function. In chapter 2's exercises, you decided which roles would be a good fit. But which ones would be the *best* fit? You need to understand your prospective customers' pains and difficulties and want to build a customer-centric messaging strategy that immediately connects.

Facilitator Instructions

These exercises focus on consumer insight and empathy. You'll need to see the pain and challenges, then identify how your product or service will resolve them. This requires a much deeper understanding of the customer's perspective and emotional state. Your products and services promise to fix a problem the customer feels before your brand changes how they feel once they adopt it. You can expect several layer shifts as you moderate these exercises.

- The roles participants initially identify as a priority may change.
- There will be similarities in how different roles feel before your product or service and how they feel after becoming

customers. This might influence both your messaging and your product positioning. Don't resist this.

- The features may creep into the conversation and discussion – which is okay – but this should not be used as a substitute for the content on the templates.

Step-by-Step Guidelines

In chapter 2, you identified priority audiences. In this session, we look a little more deeply at the priority audiences and gain better consumer insight into their world so we can determine how to target messages to them. This is a card-sorting exercise where participants will identify and prioritize the roles they see as the best fit. On the surface, it appears as if this task is about narrowing down the existing audiences. However, it is not an elimination exercise. It is a customer-centric alignment exercise.

10 minutes

1. Provide index cards or post-it notes to each participant. Each card or post-it should have one role written on it. These can be the roles identified and agreed to in chapter 2.
2. Expect new roles to be identified. You can even prompt participants to think outside the box if you believe they are missing positions. At this point, keep job roles open, as many roles will be eliminated or consolidated during the workshop.

15 minutes

3. One person takes their turn and lists their roles. As they do, they start to add to a matrix.

- As you add roles to the whiteboard/PowerPoint matrix, you can consolidate any duplicates. Be sure to ask permission from the group before doing so. Sometimes they will be the same, and other times, very subtle distinctions surface that helps you to see bias more clearly from a corporate perspective or critical triggers that lead to situations that make your product or service a spectacular fit.
- This will start some good conversations – remember there is no need to make final decisions.

What To Do Next

Now

- As you continue exercise 3.2, you'll alter both the priority of the roles and clarify the position even further – for example, the role of "Mom" or "College student" may become "New Mom" or "Recent graduate." Photograph the whiteboard (or save the PowerPoint slide if used) to keep a record of this point of the process.
- Are there roles missing? Sometimes participants have a card or strongly believe in a role that is not listed, but they are wary of mentioning it. Encourage them to address (or readdress) roles that have been considered not viable but may be perfect.
- Leave room for switching priorities and the opportunity to collapse roles. If you are working in PowerPoint, duplicate this slide so you can return to this view if you need to start again.

Later

- If you can't continue exercise 3.2 as a group session, you can conduct 3.2 with a smaller group or on your own. However, it will need feedback from others before a final priority customer is determined.

Exercise 3.1: Templates and Examples

- **Figure 13:** Template for Advanced Customer Empathy Insight Matrix™
- **Figure 14:** Template for Exercise 3.1 Advanced Customer Empathy Insight Matrix™ Exploring B2B and B2C Customers
- **Figure 15:** Template for Advanced Customer Empathy Insight Matrix™ for either B2B or B2C with Priority
- **Figure 16:** Example of Exercise 3.1 Advanced Customer Empathy Insight Matrix™

Figure 13: Template for Advanced Customer Empathy Insight Matrix™

	Role	Role	Role	Role
Emotional Environment				
Crisis Point				
Belief				
What is the hurt?				
What will make it better?				
How do they feel now?				
How do they want to feel?				

This matrix allows you to better understand your consumer by looking at them with empathy and compassion. What is it like for them on an emotional level, and what can your brand do to help?

Figure 14: Template for Exercise 3.1 Advanced Customer Empathy Insight Matrix™ Exploring B2B and B2C Customers

	B2B		B2C		
	Role	Role	Role 1	Role 2	Add as many roles as you need
Emotional Environment					
Crisis Point					
Belief					
What is the hurt?					
What will make it better?					
How do they feel now?					
How do they want to feel?					

Use this generic grid if you believe you have both B2B and B2C roles. Keep these two paths in the same overall grid but within different sections.

Figure 15: Template for Advanced Customer Empathy Insight Matrix™ for either B2B or B2C with Priority

Which role(s) should be the highest priority? →	Add Priority Here	Add Priority Here	Add Priority Here	Add Priority Here	Add Priority Here
	Role	Role	Role	Role	Role
Emotional Environment					
Crisis Point					
Belief					
What is the hurt?					
What will make it better?					
How do they feel now?					
How do they want to feel?					

This is the same as Figure 13, except we add priorities above the roles. You, or together with your team, determine which role is the #1 priority,

Figure 16: Example of Exercise 3.1 Advanced Customer Empathy Insight Matrix™ Exploring B2B and B2C Customers

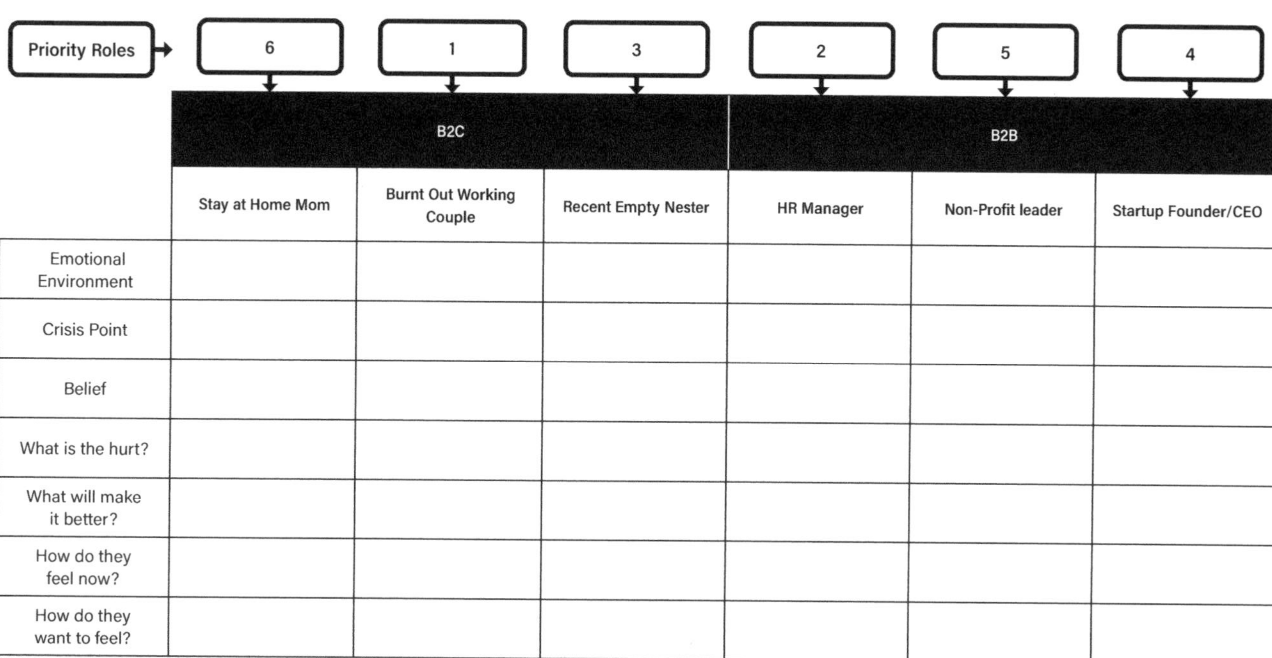

Priority Roles	6	1	3	2	5	4
	B2C			B2B		
	Stay at Home Mom	Burnt Out Working Couple	Recent Empty Nester	HR Manager	Non-Profit leader	Startup Founder/CEO
Emotional Environment						
Crisis Point						
Belief						
What is the hurt?						
What will make it better?						
How do they feel now?						
How do they want to feel?						

Here is an example of a new client trying to enter the market using both a B2C and B2B approach. There is an overlap between business and personal life. A burnout working couple may each be underperforming at their jobs. The HR manager may recognize a need to fix the corporate culture. In this example, the client is trying to determine how to enter the market. Do they go the B2B route focusing on HR programs or the B2C route focusing on couples who are burnt out and looking to relieve the pressure, stress, and difficulty? As you move forward, filling in the grid, good discussions can help create a strong market entry story.

Exercise 3.2: What Is The Need And Circumstances?

Timeframe

25 minutes

Focus

Consumer Insight | Empathy | Market Entry

Participant Instructions

While we are looking at the roles, let's focus on the human being in that role. This is an empathy exercise designed to help participants understand the people who occupy this role. Focus on a person's current circumstances that make them a prime prospective customer. The content you apply should be relevant to what you offer. It is not meant to be a complete consumer insight exercise but an investigation of the circumstances that might lead this person to seek or adopt your products or services.

Facilitator Instructions

Limit your work to the first three rows: Current environment, Crisis Point, and Belief. Depending on your participants, you can either moderate this discussion or have the content pre-filled and use it as a baseline for participants' feedback. Limit feedback to the current offer and not on potential future developments.

Step-by-Step Guidelines

Initially, it can be slow going until you get in the groove. This is not a complete consumer insight exercise – you can do that research after you have completed this chapter. Instead, focus on identifying circumstances that may lead this person to seek or adopt your products or services.

1. You will work with the participants to fill in the grid. Ask participants to take a moment to think of one of the roles. It is helpful to think of a person you know who is in that role. Ask for input on the person's environment.

♥ **Note:** *Initially, you may need to be very descriptive. As you continue, the descriptions should become concise. It is sometimes helpful to think of this as a screenplay – how would you quickly describe the role so most audience members would recognize the character?*

   - Read the description of what you are looking for.
     - The current environment is the immediate circumstances causing this person pressure or stress. The person may not know that your products or services could solve it, but they are at least considering a solution.
   - The crisis point is the moment in the person's work or personal life when they would be open to looking for a solution. People have these moments all the time.
   - The belief is the first internal alarm that says, 'there must be a better solution.

2. At this stage, you can eliminate a role. Or that a position is like another role and can be combined. For example, an HR manager and a culture officer may perform the same role if you sell to small businesses but different if you sell to mid-sized to large companies.

What To Do Next

Now

- Continue with exercise 3.3

Exercise 3.2: Templates and Examples

- **Figure 17:** Template: Advanced Customer Empathy Insight Framework™: Environment, Crisis, and Belief
- **Figure 18:** Definitions: Advanced Customer Empathy Insight Framework™—: Environment, Crisis, and Belief
- **Figure 19:** Example of Exercise 3.2 Advanced Customer Empathy Insight Matrix™: Environment, Crisis Point, and Belief

Figure 17: Template for Advanced Customer Empathy Insight Framework™ Environment, Crisis, and Belief

	Role 1	Role 2	Role 3	Role 4	Role 5
Emotional Environment					
Crisis Point					
Belief					
What is the hurt?					
What will make it better?					
How do they feel now?					
How do they want to feel?					

This is the same as Figure 15 but with the top section highlighted. It is easier to focus on building this diagram in sections.

Figure 18: Definitions of Advanced Customer Empathy Insight Framework™ Environment, Crisis, and Belief

Emotional Environment	The immediate life scenario is causing enough pain that a solution is needed, but they may not know the best solution.
Crisis Point	The troubling, uncomfortable trigger, habit, action/inaction that you could connect your product or service to as a possible solution.
Belief	What they tell themselves about how they got into this situation or believed was acceptable, but no longer is.

Figure 19: Example of Exercise 3.2 Advanced Customer Empathy Insight Matrix™ Environment, Crisis Point, and Belief

	Stay at Home Mom	Working Couple	Midlife Crisis	Workaholic (manager or exec)	HR Managers	Non Profit Leaders
Emotional Environment	Children (any age) on edge of divorce	Edge of divorce each is apathetic	A Wake-up call that can't be ignored	Self-sabotage behavior impacting life and relationships	Discrepancy between work, culture ,and policy	'Justifiable' calling is more important than family
Crisis Point	Workaholic partner is not part of family	Awareness they are using (something) to numb life	Empty nester/ recently laid-off/ new health scare/destructive coping behavior	Isolated/ feeling empty	Can't attract or keep top talent. Missing performance KPIs	Sacrifice to do good is leading to burn out and community decline
Belief	Relationships based on workaholic belief system	This is what is expected to get ahead	My bad choices caused this.	Constant cycle of Stress/perform/ achieve	Balanced culture will lead to innovation and profit	Relationships based on 'Service Above All" belief

This example comes from a firm with products and services that help people whose life experience is suffering from poor work/personal boundaries.

Exercise 3.3: What Do They Want to Feel?

Timeframe

40 minutes

Focus

Consumer Insight | Empathy | Market Entry

Participant Instructions

This is a continuation of the Customer Empathy Insight Framework. In this exercise, you are getting deeper into what your customer needs to build a relationship with you. Stay focused on one role at a time. You'll work on that role and then move to the next one.

Facilitator Instructions

This time, limit your work to the last four rows: what is the hurt, what will make it feel better, how do they feel now, and how do they want to feel? Depending on your participants, you can either moderate this discussion or have them fill the content in. Keep the feedback focused on the current offer and not on future developments.

Step-by-Step Guideline

10 minutes

1. **What is the hurt?** This simple question is aimed at getting to your customer's core issue. It isn't their entire life, but it is the issue they are facing that you could solve. From the customer's perspective, what would they say about themselves?

10 minutes

2. **What will make it better?** This usually includes the alternatives that this customer may consider or find while talking with others or researching a solution. This section has a profitable outcome, in that it can often be an inspiration and resource for content, tools, onboarding, or new services you can offer.

10 minutes

3. **How do they feel now?** Pinpoint the negative emotion they feel now. If you could only choose one emotion, which one would be most appropriate? This step will provide the language used to attract customers in need (in other words, they have the pain and current feeling) and help sales to ask questions to expose how complex the issues are for prospective customers. It's a critical point that allows you fully understand and connect with customers because you see them and know how they feel. This builds a level of trust from which a relationship can begin.

10 minutes

4. **How do they want to feel?** Identify the positive emotion using the emotional wheel: think about the emotional journey you are promising your customer. If the customer uses your products or services, how will you transport them from emotional need to emotional fulfillment? How do you make the bad feelings go away? Can your customer shift from anxious/worried to happy/proud/confident? How about from fear/anxious/concerned to surprised/excited/energetic? To

truly connect, you must prove you hear your audience. You empathize with them. You know how they feel and see the relief they seek. When you do that, you can break through the noise. Your audience feels heard, seen, and recognized. They turn to you. You believe them. And they will follow.

Note: *You should print out or project a color version of the emotional wheel (see example further down in this chapter). It is helpful if participants can physically hold the wheel in their hands – then they can twist and turn it as they answer.*

What To Do Next

Now

- The content collected from the collaboration with the participants in exercises 3.2 and 3.3 is an excellent starting point. It represents people's lives – what they are experiencing. Photograph or save the content on the whiteboards (or PowerPoint) as your baseline.
- In a minor group session or on your own, fine-tune the grid content, so it truly represents a person at a point in their life. At this point, don't try to enrich the content so that your brand will fit; stay true to representing the person. You don't want every role to be your best customer. This is a selection process through which we will leave some customers aside, to focus on the best scenario in which your brand can begin a relationship.
- As you home in on the customers, you can't help but see the power of what your brand can do when you look at it from this empathetic point of view.

Later

- Continue with Chapter 4.

Exercise 3.3: Templates and Examples

- **Figure 20:** Exercise 3.3 Advanced Customer Empathy Insight Matrix™: The Hurt, Make it Better, Feel Now, Want to Feel
- **Figure 21 Definitions:** Advanced Customer Empathy Insight Matrix™: The Hurt, Make it Better, Feel Now, Want to Feel
- **Figure 22:** Example of Advanced Customer Empathy Insight Matrix™: The Hurt, Make it Better, Feel Now, and Want to Feel Sections
- **Figure 23:** The Emotional Wheel Chart

**Figure 20: Exercise 3.3 Advanced Customer Empathy Insight Matrix™
The Hurt, Make it Better, Feel Now, Want to Feel.**

Priority Roles	Role 1	Role 2	Role 3	Role 4	Role 5	Role 6
Emotional Environment						
Crisis Point						
Belief						
What is the hurt?						
What will make it better?						
How do they feel now?						
How do they want to feel?						

This grid is the same as Figure 17 but with the lower section highlighted. You want to focus on building this diagram in sections or all at once.

Figure 21 Definitions: Advanced Customer Empathy Insight Matrix™ The Hurt, Make it Better, Feel Now, Want to Feel

What is the hurt?	The emotion behind a typical objective
What will make it better?	Known or familiar issue customer knows they need help to address.
How do they feel now?	Headline messaging that would grab attention.
How do they want to feel?	The emotional outcome of your value promise.

Figure 22: Example of Advanced Customer Empathy Insight Matrix™ The Hurt, Make it Better, Feel Now, and Want to Feel Sections

Priority Roles	Stay at Home Mom	Working Couple	Midlife Crisis	Workaholic (manager or exec)	HR Managers	Non Profit Leaders
What is the hurt?	Not respected and lost my voice	Feel isolated	Sense that time is running out	It's never enough no matter how much I work	Don't trust work/ life balance will get results	My pain is not as important
What will make it better?	Presence and availability of partner Respect: Saying Home IS a Job	Establish boundaries A way to reconnect Slow down	Set priorities Permanent reset Health	Know what is reasonable Set realistic boundaries Reclaim values	Define workaholic culture Train managers to set expectations	Redefine identity, worth, and work Establish realistic boundaries
How will they feel now?	Lonely	Pressured	Numb	Out of control	Overwhelmed	Disillusioned
What They Will Feel	Valued	Loving	Hopeful	Frustrated	Respected	Inspired

Use the emotional wheel to identify how they feel now and what they will feel if they are to use your products/ services.

Figure 22 is an example of a firm that helps people who have struggled with work/personal boundaries.

Figure 23: The Emotional Wheel Chart

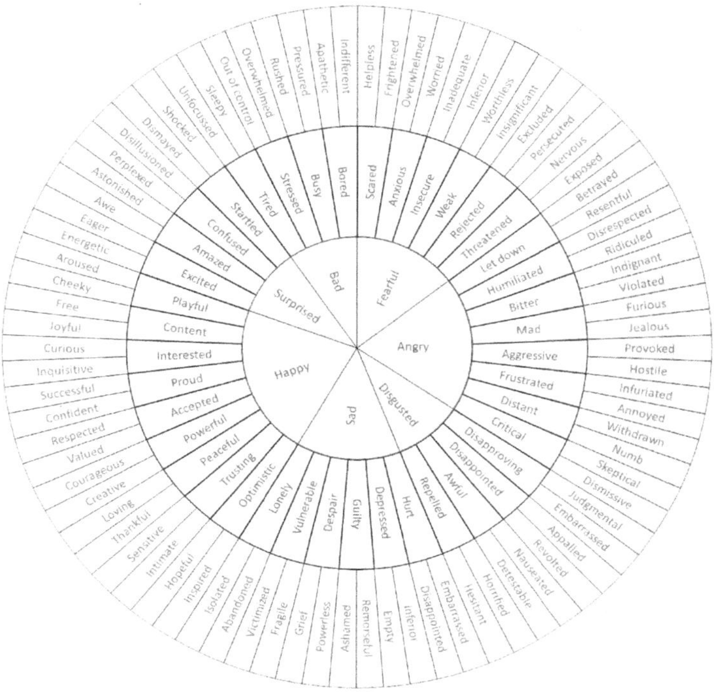

This is one example of the emotional wheel chart. You can search for others. It is very helpful to allow each participant to have a printed version of this during the workshop. This Emotional Wheel is an adaptation of *Mike Bostock's adaptation* of *Geoffrey Roberts's Emotion Wheel* using D3's *partition layout*. Robert's 2015 work appears to be based on a vocabulary wheel by *Kaitlin Robbs* from 2014, which in turn seems to be based on *The Feeling Wheel* published by Gloria Willcox in 1982.

The Client Story

If You Can't Keep Your Brand Promise to a Customer, Should They Be Your Customer?

While these exercises can be used for sizeable B2B and B2C companies, it is also relevant for smaller businesses looking to grow. A great example is work done with celebrities and authors to expand their business. It's a significant shift from a published book to consulting, workshops, and speaking engagements. Is the audience for a book the same as one who hires a keynote speaker or corporate workshop? Not always. Any extension of the book will have different audiences. It requires an intense look at who they might be and what they need. One example is a TEDx speaker and author who published a personal book on how he faced burnout. The book argues that work/life balance is a myth. Rather than balance, he advocated establishing and keeping boundaries.

While the author identified many potential audiences – who could use better work/life boundaries – we needed to understand which audience(s) made the most sense. We needed people who would recognize themselves in the book. By its very nature, the work/life boundaries story fell at the intersection of business and personal – a duality replicated in our messaging workshop.

To prioritize the right audiences, we spent time finding similarities and differences. Potential audiences can be deconstructed to include the circumstances, pressures, and stressors creating the wants and needs. We helped identify the potential target customers' environment, crisis points, and beliefs. While this exercise still didn't provide a target customer, it did allow us to see what each potential customer might be thinking and experiencing. But we needed to know what they would most value – value so much it would trigger behavior designed to stop experiencing their current situation and pain.

Part of getting deeper insight is seeing how you can help people change. You can't just attach demographics and research findings to a buyer persona template. Doing that is like playing with Colorforms™ – connecting given shapes magically to a scenic board. You need to uncover the truth about what the potential customers are facing and who may be in the right mindset to consider, trial, adopt, and champion a new approach. In this case, a book would be the basis for new in-person and digital experiences that could help people lead more fulfilling lives.

Figures 3.2 and 3.3 help show the potential audiences with specific questions related to emotional, mental, and decision-making. You don't need research to answer these questions. But you can't just copy and paste your way through this grid. This is about compassion. It's about taking a walk in someone else's shoes. It's about seeing how ready your audience might be. In this case, it is about a reader's desire to do more – to go beyond the book and extend the experience. These questions show you who to help and allow you to see what they might need from you.

Figure 24: Example of a Completed Advanced Customer Empathy Insight Matrix™

	Stay at Home Mom	Working Couple	Midlife Crisis	Workaholic (manager or exec)	HR Managers	Non Profit Leaders
Emotional Environment	Children (any age) on edge of divorce	Edge of divorce each is apathetic	A Wake-up call that can't be ignored	Self-sabotage behavior impacting life and relationships	Discrepancy between work, culture ,and policy	'Justifiable' calling is more important than family
Crisis Point	Workaholic partner is not part of family	Awareness they are using (something) to numb life	Empty nester/ recently laid-off/ new health scare/destructive coping behavior	Isolated/ feeling empty	Can't attract or keep top talent. Missing performance KPIs	Sacrifice to do good is leading to burn out and community decline
Belief	Relationships based on workaholic belief system	This is what is expected to get ahead	My bad choices caused this	Constant cycle of Stress/perform/ achieve	Balanced culture will lead to innovation and profit	Relationships based on 'Service Above All" belief
What is the Hurt	Not respected and lost my voice	Feel isolated	Sense that time is running out	It's never enough no matter how much I work	Don't trust work/ life balance will get results	My pain is not as important
What Will Make it Better	Presence and availability of partner Respect: Saying Home IS a Job	Establish boundaries A way to reconnect Slow down	Set priorities Permanent reset Health	Know what is reasonable Set realistic boundaries Reclaim values	Define workaholic culture Train managers to set expectations	Redefine identity, worth, and work Establish realistic boundaries
How They Feel Now	Lonely	Pressured	Numb	Out of control	Overwhelmed	Disillusioned
What They Will Feel	Valued	Loving	Hopeful	Frustrated	Respected	Inspired

The content in this grid is powerful stuff. From a messaging perspective, it can form the basis of campaigns. You can see how you'd capture customers' attention at their trigger/crisis points. The threads of the emotional angle of the creative campaign are there. You can imagine articles, ads, and podcasts for each audience. Moreover, you can start to see which of these customers it will make the most sense to focus on as you extend the brand and those who aren't aligned.

For the client, the grid helps eliminate audiences right away. The non-profit leaders and college deans didn't have a strong response to the question of "What they feel now" to which we could seek a solution. The Senior HR managers/well-being officer did feel overwhelmed, but when you looked at the question "What will make it better?" there is significant competition in this space. For example, "Defining a workaholic culture" would be a long-term shift and involve more than what the client could provide as part of their brand.

The Stay as Home Mom was also not a primary audience. The Working Couple and Workaholic Manager were seen as a related audience. They shared common feelings that are hard to sustain without seeking help: The manager feels "out of control/frustrated," and the working couple feels "pressured." Their answers to "What will make it better?" also aligned with products and services available at launch: podcasts, articles, speaking engagements on topics related to "setting and establishing boundaries," finding "ways to start talking as a couple, and "knowing what is reasonable." These elements from the book can be extended to these audiences, but in media and formats that can match the experience.

Chapter 4

Where Do You Live In Your Customer's Mind?

Key Idea

Positioning is about the strategic placement of your product or service in the customer's mind. The traditional way to develop positioning is to compare you against the competitors within your industry. This is often confused with the perception map, which is a helpful visual but one that fails to make you think about two fundamental questions: Do you even belong in this industry? Are you comparing your brand to what the customers believe or what you believe about it?

Positioning is a statement targeted to a specific demographic segment. When drafting a positioning statement, you lean on internal dialogue – the founder's vision, product team, and marketing have already decided on the positioning without ever listening to an actual customer. Brands that conduct surveys, interviews, and observations often interpret the results exactly where the positioning was envisioned the whole time. That approach is primed for confirmation bias. The saying is true: you hear what you want to hear. When you already know where you want to be, you'll find the way to get there. You may get to the position you want in your customer's mind but, in the process, you could be ignoring the signs that tell you there is a better, more lucrative, and defensible place you could be.

Identifying a stronger position, or even being open to a new customer mindset, is filled with fear: fear of thinking too far outside the box. People fear that being the first or being too different would take a significant investment. Positioning is about seeing the nuances and listening carefully to uncover the spaces where customers want a product to be but one isn't available yet. If you listen to what the customers are asking for, you may find it doesn't exist, but could if you positioned your product differently. To get your positioning right, you need the guts to listen to what the customers are asking for. You need to ask the questions that no one is asking and to hear what customers want. You already have an idea of your initial positioning, so it may be best to challenge that by pitting it against what customers might think. The real positioning question is not: "What is your positioning in your customer's mind?" The more tantalizing question is, "what is the position your customer is looking to fill?"

You need a shortcut to see if your current thinking on positioning will align with your customer's imagination. This is not about where you will position your brand but where your customers will place you in their options and decision-making process. I'll give you fair warning; this section may create temporary chaos. Do it anyway.

What Is Wrong with Current Methods?

Most marketers approach positioning by looking at where the brand is compared to the known competitors within a specific industry. Brands are heavily influenced by their strengths, resources, and capabilities compared to the alternatives. And this might be where it all goes wrong. When you are in the weeds, positioning is a comparison exercise. Asking "How is our brand different from the other brand?" keeps you from looking at the brand from the customer's perspective. Competitive thinking keeps you focused on the differences but not the value differentiators. Differences are small. Value differentiators are game changers.

Focusing on your value in the consumer's mind will allow you to explore different positioning in new categories you may not have considered. When encountering your brand, what category sort COULD the prospective customer put you in? What markets can you create that would enable your brand to be so relevant that competitors might not have a fighting chance? You want to be different. To stand out. To be the one brand that customers think of. Being different takes creativity and persuasive tactics to grab the attention of new customers. It may appear harder at first. But the time and effort of being another competitor will pale compared to being the only brand.

When Do You Need to Address This?

Work on the positioning when you can't get traction with new customers or are having difficulty transitioning existing customers to new products, services, or offerings. It is also an excellent aspect of your business to reevaluate when you are in a pricing war, and the margins are thin. You may not have the resources, capability, or even the energy required to stay in a highly competitive space. It might be time to shift the position.

Poor Lead Generation

Do you have limited click-through rates and highly competitive keywords? Are vastly different products and services being seen on Search Engine Results Pages (SERP)? If enough of the leads that make it through are not what you actually offer, this would also be a danger sign that you should reconsider your positioning.

High Bounce Rates

If the performance of your campaigns and website doesn't result in any reasonable engagement, even with all your attempts to fix it by tweaking content and A/B testing variations, it's time to rethink the positioning. If there is a big disconnect between what you are offering and what your audience believes you're offering, there is an alignment problem that requires a look at the positioning.

Difficult Customer Acquisition

When the consumer compares you to competitors, they may not quite believe in the value of your brand or understand what makes you different. If the positioning is based on differences, the initial sales may be lower as you work to prove you belong in the game.

Why Doing This Now Will Get You a Better ROI

Many people may believe they don't have the funds or time to create a market. That may have been a valid idea years ago when brands needed resources to fund market disruption. Now, consumers are part of your marketing team. Social networks, influencers, content creators, and the immediacy of market feedback mean early customers reward brands that disrupt markets with innovative products and services. Customers know when they have found something that fulfills them. The product or service and the experience feel "just right" and somehow something they have always wanted. It is such a novel feeling that customers can't help themselves – they need to share their joy using their platforms. As marketers, it is our responsibility to encourage our customers to spread the word. We give them bragging rights that they have discovered something new, different, and vital to their life. The ROI of finding your market rather than fighting for a place in an existing market is the sweetness of having no relevant competitors. Competitive positioning is about the question of how you compare with other alternatives in an existing market. Unique positioning is the market you create **with your customers**. It is all about finding **your** market with customers and owning it.

How To Fix It - Workshops and Exercises

What Is the Actual Value?

Two exercises build positioning based on value from the customers' viewpoint. In this exercise, you will listen differently. Rather than connecting what you have with what the customer says, the intention is to just listen to what customers would genuinely value. You will develop a customer-centric competitive positioning statement by building a customer value framework. This customer value framework will help to define what your product positioning is. This is a bottom-up approach that allows you to see the brand from the front line. The question to ask is, "What do your customers value?"

The framework will then be used to develop or alter your positioning statement and influence your messaging strategy. Building the customer-centric framework will require an interim step – comparing it to your competitor's positioning to identify the differentiators. The aim is to either confirm you have it right or highlight areas where facts, opinions, and sentiments may have been ignored. Remember, positioning is the space you take up in your customer's mind. This section will focus on knowing what it is or could be.

Because positioning is related to value proposition, the first exercise examines precisely what the customer would most value. It won't be a single feature and benefit: it will be a set of values that the customer will receive – and the order of these values is essential. This is the time to think about importance. You can offer something like a competitor, but how you bundle it or the weight you give towards a specific component makes a critical difference.

Remain in the customer's perspective. Your responses must be based on what THEY value.

Remember to think about values and not your features and benefits. Don't worry. There will be a chance to tout your features and benefits is coming in a future chapter. For now, focus on the value your products and services provide. For this exercise, we can think of importance in these terms:

- A fundamental belief or process that helps people function as a team
- A tool, system, or piece of information that allows people to work towards a common goal
- Reinforcing or systemizing guiding principles that support change
- Product or service outcomes that support business relationships, customer relationships, and company growth.

For example, if you are the manufacturer of a new handle that can be installed in a shower to help people get in and out of it, you may be inclined to say the value is:

- An easy-to-install handle that fits most showers
- A no-slip surface design for people with weaker hand grip
- It is engineered at the angle that provides the most support

But at this stage, the customer doesn't know those values. What the customer values are:

- A way to get in and out of the shower safely.

Exercise 4.1: What Is the Actual Value?

Timeframe

60 minutes

Focus

Positioning by Role | Value Identification and Prioritization | Value Framework | Design Thinking

Participant Instructions

Looking at your top target audiences, you decide what your customers value most. This can include features and functions you already have and, more importantly, what the customers are asking for. As in all exercises, you'll be challenged to think from the customer's perspective. If you have done surveys or interviews or have comments or chats from platforms, I encourage you to review them at this stage.

Facilitator Instructions

As you begin this exercise, stay true to the customer's values even if they do not exist in your current offering. Encourage participants to include what they see as the essential value and two others in the order of importance. Sometimes, people value a shift in how you present the value you already have or a value you could address, with a bit of work. If you have time beforehand, review surveys, interviews, comments, or chats from platforms, sales presentations, and customer service conversations. It may be beneficial to have quotes on hand to spark conversation or challenge the brand perspective. Before you place content on the template, be sure to discuss it. You want some agreement here.

The second exercise will allow you and the participants to explore a creative interpretation of that value. This exercise helps you see short-term ways to shift your offer to align with your customers' wants. Sometimes it can be a simple change in the words you use – for instance, you could ask, "Do you take aspirin?" or "Do you take painkillers?" It can also be something simple, like highlighting something you already do but don't tell the customers about. This could involve adding something to your website or moving a feature of your application or onboarding process.

Step-by-Step Guideline

Using the whiteboard or PowerPoint template, list the customers in the left column. The customers should be listed from the most important at the top and the least important at the bottom. If participants keep leaning on features and benefits, it may be helpful to have pre-made cards that include the known values customers and prospects have identified.

20 minutes

1. Have participants write what customers 1, 2, and 3 would most value. Stay with the first three because there will be some changes during the discussion. It will make the exercise go faster as you proceed.
2. Stick with your brand's values and avoid defaulting to the features/benefit lingo. This exercise should focus on the importance of experiencing and interacting with the

product or service. What is the outcome of the features and benefits?

3. Give participants 3-4 minutes to fill in their post-it notes. Then begin to place them on the framework. As you do, review, and discuss until you get a strong consensus.
4. It does not matter if you have a solution for the value today; acknowledging it is more important than ignoring it.
5. Expect intense discussion and lots of movement of post-it notes.
6. Keep filling out the grid for the next three customers until you have completed the sheet.
7. Spend time editing and negotiating until you have a single item in each grid.
    - Be sure to edit or alter content if it is a specific feature and benefit, not a value

Note: *The values are often harder to articulate – especially for brands transitioning to customer-centricity and still understanding how to co-create with customers. It is equally tricky for start-ups with little data and early products. This involves acceptance of what customers need. It is market-driven, not brand-driven. You need to fulfill the market's needs better than anyone else. To do that, this understanding of value may be your best weapon.*

What To Do Next

Now

- Photograph the whiteboard as it is (or save a version of the PowerPoint slide)!
- Choose to pause or continue: This content may require polishing up before moving on to the next exercise – applying which customer value to help create a positioning

statement. You can stop here and do the following exercise with an updated version of this chart.

Later

- If you do make some changes, add a review session to get a round of feedback.
- Changes to this document outside the workshop should be influenced by direct information from the customer's perspective. Testing these values with customer interviews would not be a bad idea.

Exercise 4.1: Templates and Examples

- **Figure 25:** Customer Value Grid™ Template
- **Figure 26:** Example of Customer Value Grid™ for Working Service Dog Website
- **Figure 27 Example:** Customer Value Grid™ for Workplace Misconduct Application

Figure 25: Customer Value Grid™ Template

		What do they **COMPLETELY** value?	What do they **MOSTLY** value?	What do they **SLIGHTLY** value?
Most Important Customer	Customer 1			
↓	Customer 2			
	Customer 3			
	Customer 4			
	Customer 5			
Least Important Customer	Customer 6			

The Customer Value™ Grid provides two lines of tension. Vertically, participants need to establish the most important customers. And secondly, they need to define what and how much they value. The two issues need to be monitored as they are, by design, making you decide on an audience to focus on.

Figure 26: Example of Customer Value Grid™ for Working Service Dog Website

		What do they **COMPLETELY** value?	What do they **MOSTLY** value?	What do they **SLIGHTLY** value?
Most Important Customer	Service Dog Trainer	Confident training will help dogs graduate with right skills.	Sanctioned training harness and products dogs will need to work.	Food and treats.
↓	Service Dog Owner (certified)	A standard, recognized ID to eliminate interruption and challenges.	Register in an official database.	Products that prevent others from interfering with working dog.
↓	Therapy Support Dog Trainer	Standard training process for typical emotional needs.	Skill that can build the reputation and business.	Able to know state rights and restrictions.
↓	Therapy Support Dog Owner	Medical requirements, forms and process to qualify for therapy dogs.	Understanding of state rights and restrictions.	An official, recognized ID.
↓	Person Verifying Certification of Dog	Access to an official database to verify working dogs.	Clarify current laws by state.	An official, recognized ID.
Least Important Customer	Emotional Support Dog	Treats, scratches, lots of love.	Balance of fun with dog pals and naps.	Harness that fits well and makes me look cool.

Figure 26 helped shift the brand from individuals who wanted to obtain information on emotional support certification to dedicated service dog trainers and service dog owners. This shifted the digital experience and content to focus on the most valuable customers and what THEY needed.

Figure 27: Example of Customer Value Grid™ for Workplace Misconduct Application

		What do they **COMPLETELY** value?	What do they **MOSTLY** value?	What do they **SLIGHTLY** value?
Most Important Customer ↓	Whistleblower	Safe reporting tool	A standard private investigation process.	A corporate culture where input matters
	CEO	Control culture	Able to take action early.	Protect company.
	HR Manager	A standard private investigation process | know what to do	Not missing something important.	Retraining to fix lack of understanding.
	Corporate Lawyer	Keep data internal	Protect company	A standard private investigation process.
	Board of Directors	Protect Company	Understand benchmark of peers.	Company is compliant.
Least Important Customer	Prospective Employees	A corporate culture where input matters.		

Figure 27 shows the potential target customers and what they value for a workplace misconduct application.

Exercise 4.2: How Does the Customer Experience the Value?

Timeframe

45 minutes

Focus

Value Alignment | Digital Experience

Participant Instructions

This is a design thinking exercise. It requires NO drawing or fancy design training. It requires you to draw a schematic. You can choose one of four options:

- A homepage for your website
- A landing page for the product
- A mobile application dashboard
- The initial screens of an onboarding process

Facilitator Instructions

You should choose the experience that you should be focused on.

- If your product is an application, draw the dashboard.
- If you are a service, draw a wireframe of what the audience should see – either on the homepage, landing page, product detail page, or a kiosk – whichever experience makes sense.
- If you want a free trial of a new product, start with the onboarding process.

Step-by-Step Guideline

15 minutes

1. You are drawing a schematic focused on embedding the value into the experience. It is vital that customers feel the value immediately. The size and placement of the boxes should represent the importance of the value, and the interaction/experience/message should reinforce the value. You want to include a keyword or phrase on the box or circle, so we know what it represents.
2. This is much more about emphasizing where it belongs – on the customer value and not on your features, benefits, or the brand's perspective. The relative placement of the content and the size of the area are far more critical than the "design."
3. Paper and markers or crayons are recommended.

15 minutes

4. Have each participant review their design. Participants can just walk through want they did. There is no need for criticism of the work product. Positive reinforcement is encouraged.
5. If a senior person is in the room, starting with someone with a minor tenure who is closer to the customer/prospects might be best.
6. Each participant can review their work; naturally, there will be some positive discussion and good-natured fun.

15 minutes

7. Continue with a collaborative session to identify the vital components. It might be that each participant brought value to the experience, or a few nailed it. What is important here is that the discussion is based on the best or better ideas that came from this and NOT on the participant's role, experience, or talents.
8. Be sure to capture this collaboration – **it can be used to develop a prototype.**

What To Do Next

Now

- If the order of the values you identified on the schematics differs from those in exercise 4.1, you must resolve this discrepancy. You can choose to reorganize the components in the sketches, OR you can alter the content in the Customer Value Template. The customer must experience the value directly, intuitively, and unconsciously.
- If the values on the wireframes and the Customer Value template align, you can move on to testing this value further by drafting a positioning statement.

Later

- Creating a more formal schematic that collects the values you and the participants discussed is a great tool for sharing the direction and commitment to embedding the value into the engagement. At this stage, it doesn't require a designer; it can just be a cleaned-up version using PowerPoint or Keynote. Sharing the schematic with the value narrative is a powerful way to structure the experience based on a valuable connection.

- When you're ready, a UX/UI designer can take your schematic and work their magic to turn it into a glorious experience.

Exercise 4.2: Templates and Examples

- **Figure 28:** Example of Customer Value Wireframe for Service Dog Site

Figure 28: Example of Customer Value Wireframe for Service Dog Site

Customer Value Wireframe: This is just a rough drawing. You need to ensure that the items you are adding are what customers

Exercise 4.3: A Quick Positioning Statement

Timeframe

20 minutes

Focus

Value Alignment | Positioning Statement

Participant Instructions

This quick "back of an envelope" exercise stretches the values and experience and rolls it up to the positioning statement. It is about testing your commitment to customer-centricity by constraining the positioning statement to be based on the customer's perspective. These statements are never easy or quick. Given the work you have just done in this mindset, ask yourself again, what is our positioning statement?

Facilitator Instructions

Bridging the gap between a workshop experience focused on value and the positioning statement is an important exercise to do now. While the participants are thinking from the customer's perspective, with their values sitting front and center, try to write a positive statement that is saturated with customer values. Watch out for conversations that drift back to the older positioning or resistance to staying focused on the target customers they just agreed to!

♥ *My favorite positioning statement book is Crossing the Chasm* **by Geoffrey Moore**.

Step-by-Step Guideline

The act of defining what customers value leads us to a place where we should be able to understand the impact of our decisions. While you are deep into thinking from the customer's perspective, it is time to look at your positioning. Doing this now may feel like a jolt to your work. However, this is one of those situations where all of you are in a new mindset – and you can use this ability to see yourself differently. It is a chance to acknowledge what this would mean about your positioning in the market. It may be a small change or a significant one. This is an opportunity to see what you could be now.

20 minutes

1. Your task is to write a new positioning statement.
    - You can choose to review your current positioning statement with the value framework completed in exercise 4.1 or use this framework to help craft a new one that you can compare to your old positioning.
2. Follow either positioning template 1 or 2 by inserting content based on the workshop work you have done.
    - This exercise seems easy, but it can be difficult to choose words that your brand will need to live with. The pressure will mount. Stress will set in. But believe in the work you are doing to bring the customer into the room. Stay focused on being extremely valuable.
    - You'll find yourself returning to other components each time you change one section. This is just how it goes. It can feel like you are making trade-offs as

you define what you offer and who wants it. And that is the point.

What To Do Next

Now

- If you exceed 20 minutes, it is okay. This can take a lot of work to get right.
- Photograph the whiteboard or PowerPoint as it is.
- Put a draft of the positioning statement on the wall and leave it there. It will take time and several iterations to get this polished. Also, it's helpful if it can stay in the conference room or open space so others can look at it in passing. You'll find you start making minor adjustments to every part of it – it is like straightening a crooked picture frame. You see it, and you can't help but walk over and fix the alignment.

Later

- You should save a copy for other exercises. This "current positioning statement" will probably need another look and potential adjustments as you continue with the next chapter. The good news is that its current form is based on a customer's perspective. So, congratulations!

Exercise 4.3: Templates and Examples

- **Figure 29:** Templates: Positioning Statement Formula and YOUR Customer Value
- **Figure 30:** Template: Customer Value Grid™

Figure 29: Templates for Positioning Statement Formula and YOUR Customer Value

Traditional Positioning Statement Formula Template 1

To____________ (target), your product/service is the

_________________(category) that

__________________________ (unique benefit) that's

because ____________________ (supporting

points/compelling evidence)

Traditional Positioning Statement Formula Template 2

To ___________________ (target customers) who

_________________ (statement of the need or opportunity), the

_______________________ (product name) is a

_______________________ (product category) that

______________________ (statement of key benefit) that is

________________________ (compelling reason to buy).

Figure 29 shows two positioning statements are examples. Pick one or find another that you prefer. The challenge is to fill it in using the content from a customer-centric perspective.

Figure 30: Template for Customer Value Grid™

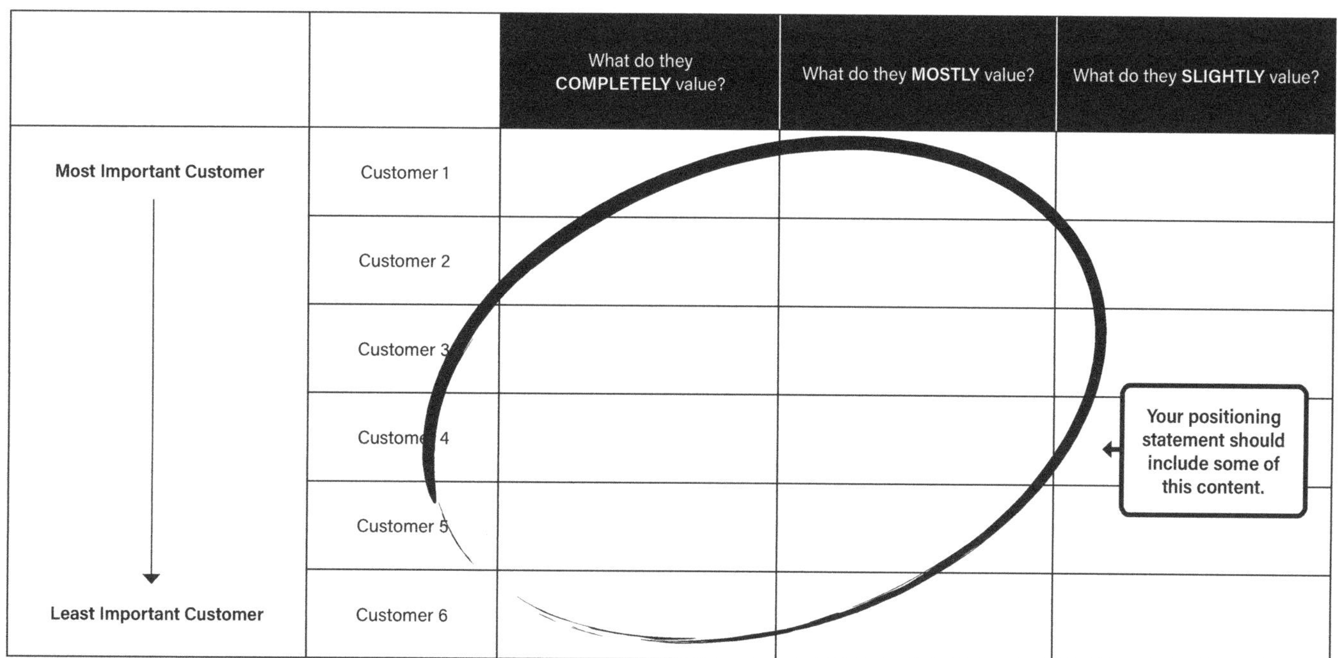

Customer Value Template: The work you agreed on the Customer Value Grid should be used to influence your positioning statement. These are your target customers, and this is what they value.

The Client Story

When Is A Market Ready For Disruption?

One client with first-hand experience of discrimination in the workplace launched an application to address problems with reporting, investigating, and resolving harassment, discrimination, and suspicious behavior. Workplace discrimination and harassment is a complex process handled differently from company to company. Errors, delays, and ignoring complaints resulted in an increase in more severe, systemic workplace harassment. In addition, senior management had been responsible for an inadequate response which had resulted in stock market price declines and a series of CEOs being fired.

During the market research stage, it was discovered that employees feared retaliation from reporting and were often ignored, even when there was substantial evidence. Research also showed that employees wanted to report inappropriate actions because they wanted to work in a culture that treats people fairly. Part of the problem was that the process to report and manage reporting discrimination was different across organizations and could shift based on who was leading the investigation, who was involved, and how severe it was. The number and variability of people, departments, and regulations made a difficult situation more complex, and the response was inconsistent and often inadequate. The start-up needed to understand who would gain the most value with their product to launch a new methodology. The start-up also realized that a standardized, best-practice process would provide a more consistent approach and outcomes that would improve employees' confidence that reports would be managed without retaliation.

For this disruptive start-up that addressed a cultural issue, getting into the specifics of what each audience would value helped to prioritize the go-to-market strategy and to define and elevate the messaging for multiple stakeholders.

The Audience Value Framework allowed the start-up team to home in on what was necessary for each audience and helped bring new appealing messages shared by multiple internal stakeholders to the surface. In this framework, the audiences are listed on the left in the order of priority. In this case, a reporter is someone submitting a report, whether they are a witness or a victim. Along the top are three values. They are listed as being of high, moderate, and low significance. The values are NOT features, benefits, or practices that exist – although some may exist. The values are meant to discover what MUST be present to make a difference for the related audience stakeholders.

In this case, three messaging themes surfaced. Each message was on a high or moderate level for the prioritized audiences:

Primary Shared Values

- A standard private investigation process
- Protect the company
- Clarify what happened

Secondary Shared Values

- Know what to do
- Act quickly

Those primary shared value messages were universal to the marketing and sales of the product. Together with the secondary shared values, they differentiated this product against existing solutions and internal processes. When compared to competitors, the combination of shared values was a defensible position. It was also clear to see these and realize that this was a fundable start-up. This resolved a problem that no other current product or service could. The shared values allowed audience members to see their current situation as lacking. You can imagine an organization saying, "we have an investigation process, but it's not always followed, and there have been problems with privacy." You can also easily see a connection with the need to "clarify what happened." Tools like whistleblower hotlines and the reluctance of reporters to use an email address that may be linked to their identity support the need to explain what happened.

In conversations with early potential customers, knowing what to do to "protect the company" was crucial. Each prospective customer could point to situations in which this knowledge had been lacking. There was also a shared interest in handling complaints in a way that protected the company from being seen as having a bad culture that did not protect its employees. See Figure 27 for the sample from this client story.

Chapter 5

What Is Your Emotional Promise?

Key Idea

When Marshall McLuhan wrote, "the medium is the message," he wanted to convey the symbiotic relationship created when the medium itself influences the perception of the message. For me, the messaging is not the words, tone, or images – it is the creation of the entire digital experience. The message is built on an information architecture with a clear hierarchy – with the most important elements at the top. The information architecture dictates the digital experience of the messages. It helps you to design emotional and intellectual connections.

The expression "transportation" describes what it feels like when you get lost in a book. This kind of "transportation" can also occur with a well-crafted digital experience that takes the customer on an internal emotional transition in which they shift to believing in you and your brand. The adventure takes them out of themselves. In a great digital experience, customers become enthralled and attentive to you, because the digital experience is captivating – it feels right, and precisely what they need. Your message is not the words or pictures but the entire digital experience. They are not separate components.

Creating a captivating digital experience that is also the message requires you to think of messaging as engagement. Engagement is designed to create a feeling of transportation. The digital experience is comprised of anything the customer interacts with. It can be a single landing page, a social media post, a welcome email, a banner ad, a mobile application, the onboarding experience, the site navigation, multiple pieces of a marketing campaign, user-generated content, or paid and free content (such as white papers, product sheets, or how-to). The entire digital experience of your brand contributes to your messaging strategy. Individually and collectively, the components are an interpretation of the values: the manifestation of the emotional connections you are trying to solidify. Each experience must be tied to the messaging as a single component and a collective.

Unfortunately, content, campaigns, and experiences are often created as one-off elements, separately from the messaging strategy. This distance between the development of messaging and digital expertise can make it hard for marketers to pinpoint communication problems. If you are the type of marketer or founder who believes the messaging is about picking a stunning heroic image and a great headline for the homepage, along with a big "buy now" button, then you will be on a slower path to growth. Suppose you're willing to see your messaging strategy as foundational to the digital experience. In that case, you'll develop expertise based on genuine connections to loyal customers and influencers rather than the conversion of a few users. The messaging must be built into the information flow, navigation, content, images, tone, colors, graphics, forms, pop-ups, and follow-ups. The digital experience is a tangible representation of the messaging. It makes no difference if it is a website for a product or service, an application, or an onboarding process – digital engagement is the messaging, and all interactions must communicate the messaging strategy.

What Is Wrong with Current Methods?

Whether you undertake the messaging strategy as a component of your brand strategy or a new marketing campaign, the words will be carefully selected – even fought over – and they do matter. Messaging reflects your ideology, purpose, and differentiation; therefore, it is essential to be precise about who you say the brand is and what it represents. Many outcomes are created or updated from the messaging strategy, including updating the brand guide, reworking the messaging architecture, or developing a new tagline or campaign theme.

Traditionally, the branding exercise does not involve thinking about the user experience of the messaging in all its forms: words, images, content, information flow, and so on. When we get caught up in the messaging, we forget the customer's emotional state and the need to shift from where it is to what it can be. As you develop the messaging strategy, take a moment to lock in on the emotional trajectory of the customer. For example, let's say you want to open a martial arts studio. Is the martial arts studio promising to help customers have a sense of safety or allow customers the ability to protect themselves? Security and protection might feel very different from the customer's perspective. If the martial arts studio offers safety, the customer's relevant emotional state may be vulnerable, fragile, or feel threatened. Your messaging might need to help the customer feel confident or empowered. If your message is more about allowing a student to feel they can protect themselves, your customer might start out feeling weak, helpless, or nervous. In that case, your messaging needs to promise that they will feel courageous or capable.

As part of the messaging strategy within the framework of customer-centric thinking, it makes sense to explore the emotional and digital experiences while you are still working out exactly what you represent. This is a point at which you can test the difference in order to share the nuances of what you can be to your customers. There is a need to explore the emotional connection and the digital experience as a direct output of the messaging. By extending the messaging strategy to the digital experience at this early stage, you are activating design thinking – specifically, looking at scenarios to ensure the messaging is what you want AND building a path to engagement. The customers don't want to be aware of an experience; they want to be in the experience. Just think about the difference between watching people experience a roller coaster is very different from sitting in the front seat of the roller coaster.

When Do You Need to Address This?

Depending on where you are in your go-to-market strategy, you will have different points that let you know you need to focus on this issue. Indeed, the best time to do this exercise is early in the process – during the initial prototype stage. Making the direct connection between the digital experience and the emotional reaction allows for a richer engagement. If you are already in the market, you might feel like there is no lift, attention, or concentration and that prospective customers don't understand what you are offering quickly enough. If prospective customers do not actively peruse the content, there is little dialogue during initial conversations, and the hill to climb to get prospective customers to open up about their wants and needs gets steeper and steeper.

Disagreement on User Experience

This can be conflicting views on the prototype for an application, an onboarding process, or the information architecture for a new site. Often there will be tension between a utilitarian approach and one that is more emotional. Alternatively, it could be that the usability testing results are not good, and you don't know how you got it so wrong.

Extensive, Rocky Sales Cycle

It may be that prospective customers don't believe that you provide what they need and only see it after lots of questions, emails, conversations, sales presentation, demonstrations, and evaluation is completed that shows how your product or service offers what they need. If it takes a great deal of time, excessive exchange of information, and lots of clarification that only the most dedicated prospective customers are willing to do, then the problem is that they did not believe your claims to begin with. In this case, you are losing potential customers who aren't willing to go through that level of effort.

Poor User Engagement

It may be that you have little or unremarkable engagement with prospective customers who quickly abandon your website, never download free or gated content, or eliminate you from Request For Proposals (RFP) that you are qualified for. It's the lack of a good first impression that can hurt your business and bruise your brand soul. If customers and prospects don't engage, there is no basis for growing a mutually benedictional relationship. And, you are seen as not adding value.

Why Doing This Now Will Get You a Better ROI

Leading psychologists have proven that people use intuitive and emotional thinking to make quick judgments and fast decisions. Even for the critical decisions in our life, careful, deliberate thought is not always accessible. The pressures of time and the endless flow of information add layers of stress, uncertainty, and worry. Emotions play a major role in how your customers perceive problems and available solutions. If your digital experience does not match either the emotion felt when the customers have a problem or the relief they will feel when the issue is resolved, you won't connect to their emotional needs.

Based on research, nearly 95% of customers' decisions are unconscious. It is the easier, faster way of thinking. Even for business decisions that should be logical and systematic, emotions creep in. Customer often rationalize their purchasing decisions and then look for evidence to prove they are being rational. Even for complex purchases that involve larger groups of buyers, activating their emotions will work to your advantage. It will trigger the digital path your prospective customers will take to rationalize their decision. As they find the information they seek when they need it, it reinforces their original gut instinct. It can feel like a betrayal if they cannot find the information they want. Their initial trust in their instinctive gut feeling was off. They won't blame themselves. They will feel like you let them down. And they will blame you.

Customers who can make faster decisions make your sales cycle more efficient and productive. Customers with a strong, positive emotional experience are also more likely to provide recommendations, reviews, and ratings, which in turn will increase new buyers' confidence. Helping customers feel good about themselves and their decisions are financially beneficial to your business.

How To Fix It - Workshop and Exercises

What Is The Emotional Promise?

In chapter 3, we explored the way our different types of audiences and prospective customers feel as they realize they need a solution. The emotions identified in those exercises were from a consumer insight perspective. We will take a closer look at the type of emotion we want our audiences to feel as they explore and compare possible solutions. You need to thoughtfully, and intentionally create a digital experience that bridges the gap between how they think and what they will feel. They won't simply feel one emotion; it isn't simply "I'm confused." So this is about being deliberate and conscious of the way we have an impact on customers' lives in a few clicks.

This is a three-part exercise. In the first exercise, we revisit the ecosystem of audiences but look for what each one wants to feel as they journey through the brand experience. This will involve thinking about the emotion you promise and ensuring you create an experience that delivers on that promise. No two people are alike, so in this initial exercise, you'll identify a range of the experiences people might have. In the second exercise, you place a crucial feature or design element that MUST be front and center to let the customer know you get them. You'll also think about why this is important for the customer; this is another customer-centric check. You and your team need to back up your thinking with a firm answer to what it is for them.

Translating the emotional connection to the in-person and digital experience while focusing on the customer perspective is like walking a tightrope between two high-rise buildings without a net. You hold a balancing pole to lower your center of gravity, allowing you more stability as you take deliberate steps. The tightrope is the path to the customer. Think of the pole as you balance the features and content while keeping your gaze at the distant point – specifically, the customer's emotional need to engage. Finding the right balance of features and range allows you to move forward – to take delicate, deliberate steps toward the one thing that will keep you alive.

In chapter 4, exercise 2, you created a concept for a digital experience (your application or website) that would quickly let the audience know they were engaging with a brand that understands them. Remember that, in that exercise, you focused on the size, position, and types of content the audience would immediately relate to. It would signal that "you know their pain" and can address it. If you are building a website or landing page, the information architecture, navigation, content strategy, engagement, and social media content must match the value the customer is looking for. If you are producing an application, the features, functions, and content must also be EXACTLY what the audience wants, and not what you or your team think is best based purely on conviction.

In the third exercise, you'll need to answer the question, "What's in it for them." This critical question will help you transition the messaging strategy session work to the digital experience that the audience needs. When you link the high-level ideas of your content, features, navigation, and information architecture to a value, the audience can prioritize the most important differentiating criteria that will lead potential customers to choose you.

But there is a catch. The question "**Why does it matter to them?**" may shake up your previous results. It is meant to challenge your beliefs in your offer, push against the perceived value, **and get to the actual value**. When you begin to assign the value each audience member will receive from the content, features, function, or navigation, you can start to see some interesting findings. By asking, "**Why does it matter to them?**", you often identify a more substantial value for audience members who were lower on your initial priority list. Addressing this question cements the alignment of the customer's perspective with the digital experience. **You build the messaging into a digital engagement.** The audience is not just viewing your messaging and interacting with it. **They experience the value**. You need the features, functions, navigation, content, information, and design to feel just right. It must match what they are seeking – helping them feel better as they continue to pursue trust in your brand. You become relevant to them by showing you understand them. And then they will trust you.

Exercise 5.1 What Is the Emotional Promise?

Timeframe
30 minutes

Focus
Design Thinking | Information Design | User Experience

Participant Instructions
This is a promise. Not a grand brand promise but a small, pinky-swear promise. It is one you can make because you have control of your actions. Because you'll identify both the emotion and a feature or design element, you can create the experience that will fulfill your promise. Empathize with your customer. Give them a way to take small steps closer to you. And find a way to design the experience that will give them not what you want them to hear but what you need them to feel. Also, be open to changing the way the details are delivered. For example, you might want to give all the information up front, but customers like to find the answers to their questions as they think of them. So, an FAQ provides a slightly different path to the same information – and it is also more engaging because the user is seeking an answer to their driving question.

Facilitator Instruction
These two exercises tend to quickly settle on the emotions and identify an existing feature, design element, or module. There may be some instances where the components are all there but may not be in the correct order. Or the features may be available but

hidden behind a paywall that prevents new customers from an experience that would allow them to engage. Your intention may be to bring the essential pieces into the customer interaction to the surface.

More often, you will find the issue is that there needs to be a change in the in-person or digital experience to trigger engagement. Your participants might still not be familiar with how experiences evoke emotions. In addition to color, tone, words, and expressions, the information and how you interact with it are part of the emotional engagement experience.

If you have time beforehand, it may be helpful to have a list of existing features and benefits. I would have those on index cards. It may be beneficial to have a small list of interactive digital prompts with a quick explanation to allow participants to think outside the box. This is not a design exercise, although it can be helpful as a starting point. **It is more about linking the emotional hierarchy to the cognitive design of the user experience.**

Step-by-Step Guidelines

This hands-on exercise works better if participants can work individually or in smaller groups. It is better to be writing on the documents and handling the resources. The more physically interactive, the better. Give each participant a printout of the emotional map and the Reference sheet – Content and Design. It is easier to read this if you can physically turn it in, and it works better if these materials are spread out in front of people. You may also provide a printout of the PowerPoint version of the template that participants need to fill in. They can then copy the audience names from your previous work and individually fill in the emotional needs.

15 minutes

1. Ask participants to think of the audience types and choose the emotional promise customers would need if they engaged with your brand.
2. Ask, "**What is the emotional promise we give this customer**?" What will they feel as they engage with us?
   - Instruct them to write these down but not to share them just yet.
   - Remind participants to select three emotions prioritized from highest (most important) to lowest (less important but not anything to sneeze at).
   - You can use the emotion from exercise 3.3 as a starting point.

15 minutes

3. When they are ready, begin a facilitated discussion on the emotions each participant wrote down. You can start with one participant and one role where they can discuss the reason for their selection. Invite other participants to chime in. You should ask those with very different emotional trajectories and invite others to share.
4. As the discussion unfolds, a few natural outcomes transpire, examples of which might be:
   - Deeper discussion, and deeper, more nuanced emotions that seem similar but may have different meanings for some.
   - Emotions for different audiences may be traded – for example, most of the group may believe the CEO's highest emotional connection is to feel

"informed" but may agree later that the corporate lawyer needs to be informed. Is the emotional connection of the CEO the same as the corporate lawyer? If during the exercise, the corporate lawyer is also deemed to be 'informed,' go back to the CEO emotional needs. It may be that the CEO's emotional need should change to feel "in control." The emotional needs of each stakeholder are rarely the same.

- ▫ Yes, there may be an emotional connection shared across multiple audiences, but rarely would they all have the same feeling because their role and responsibility would alter their emotional connection.

What To Do Next

Now

- Photograph the whiteboard as it is. Or save the PowerPoint slide if you are using one. The emotional connection is the most challenging component to hold onto as you move toward the brand's experience. Keeping all the emotions you agreed to provide front and center is vital to a successful digital engagement.
- You can move to exercise 5.2 now or later. If moving to exercise 5.2, transfer the audience and emotions to the new template.

Later

- If you don't move immediately to 5.2, you can schedule it for a later point.
- The emotions of each audience strand need to be transferred into your core engagement pieces. It can be added to your

brand narrative and creative briefs and discussed with sales and product managers, who can validate the emotional connection and use it as part of the sales process.

Exercise 5.1: Templates and Examples

- **Figure 31:** Example of Digital Elements and the Emotional Experience They Represent
- **Figure 32:** Template for Customer Emotional Connection
- **Figure 33:** Example of Customer Emotional Connections for Workplace Misconduct Application

Figure 31: Example of Digital Elements and the Emotional Experience They Represent

Help button	I'm a bit lost and can't find my way. I'm frustrated that I can't do what I want to do and uncertain about what to do.
Search feature	I'm overwhelmed and want to find what I need faster. Where is the answer I am looking for? Am I in the right place? Is this the right solution for me?
FAQ	Surely, I am not the only one who has these questions. I don't want to feel inadequate or appear to be asking a question that I SHOULD know. I'll just verify that I am doing it right before I call, text, or message someone.
Quotes	Oh, good, I will have the experience that they had. It's good that others can confirm that this brand is good! [Or, if it is a bad review on a social site] I KNEW IT! This brand can't be trusted.
Pricing tiers comparison	I need choices on what and how to purchase. I don't need to commit to everything – especially since I will likely not USE all those features. I don't want to pay too much. I need to feel in control.
Form fields	I'm willing to share a little about myself to get what I want, but don't ask too much. I'll give it an unsubscribe later.
Sign in	I'm part of the "in" crowd. If I just sign in, I'll have exclusive access to what I need.
Paywall forms	Hmmm...How much do I want that content? Can I get it someplace else?
Feature lists	Does it have what I need? Will this give me what I want? Does this allow me to be do something I can't do now?
Progress bars	I am moving along in this task and only need a little more effort before I can be done or take a break. I don't have much more to go.
Congratulations / thank you pop-ups	Hey, I did it. I have a small, proud moment of feeling as if I accomplished something.
Prompts	I'm doing everything right!

Figure 32: Template for Customer Emotional Connection

	HIGH EMOTION	MODERATE EMOTION	LOW EMOTION
Priority Audience 1 from Exercise 3.3	As a starting point, insert the emotion you identified in Exercise 3.3 (Figure 20) to the question: How do they want to feel? ↓		
Priority Audience 2 from Exercise 3.3			
Priority Audience 3 from Exercise 3.3			
Priority Audience 4 from Exercise 3.3			
Priority Audience 5 from Exercise 3.3			

In the Customer Emotional Connection, you are trying to define the emotion the customer wants to feel as they experience your brand – either online or in person. One, some, or all the high, moderate, and low feelings will lead to a connection – the closer and faster you get to the high and moderate emotions, the better connection you'll establish. You hope the customer feels all three as they engage with you. But it can also be fine if they only feel one. When selecting the highest emotional connection, you look for the emotion that will lead to a deeper relationship. The best place to start is to pull the emotion you identified in Exercise 3.3 (Figure 20) to the question: How do they **WANT** to feel?

Figure 33: Example of Customer Emotional Connections for Workplace Misconduct Application

	HIGH EMOTION	MODERATE EMOTION	LOW EMOTION
Reporter / Whistleblower	empowered	heard	safe
CEO	In control	informed	pride
HR Manager	clarity	responsible	responsive
Corporate Lawyer	informed		
Board of Directors	control	informed	pride

Figure 33 is an example of the customer emotional connections for the workplace misconduct application. The high emotions are from to the question 'How do you want the customer to feel?' For some customers - like the corporate lawyer role -there is only one emotion. For others, there is a high emotion they are seeking followed by other emotions that may be important as they proceed. For instance, the high emotion for the Reporter/Whistleblower might be feeling "empowered," the moderate one may be feeling "heard," and the low one may be feeling "safe."

Exercise 5.2: What Are the Most Valued Features, Functions, or Services, and Why Does It Matter?

Timeframe

45 minutes

Focus

Engagement | Information Design | User Experience

Participant Instructions

Your task is to design the brand's experience based on the emotion you want the customer to experience. Rather than creating content based on the question "What does the customer need to know?", you should think about the question, "What does the customer need to feel?"

Facilitator Instruction

The average businessperson doesn't have expertise in user experience design, but there is an essential awareness of the engagement intent. Part of your facilitation may be to help surface the critical content and experiences buried deep in the customer interaction or to brainstorm how to allow the customer to get to the material that matches their emotional state.

Step-by-Step Guideline

Which feature, function, or service is the most valued thing for the user? How will you deliver the emotional connection through the way you engage with them? It can be content, design, a function, or a feature – and likely a combination of everything – but the engagement must be designed based on the emotional connection. This will be a highly debated discussion. You can use your existing application or service if there is an immediate need for the participant to attend the workshop.

While the entire brand experience is essential, there must be a core feature, function, content, or experience that supports the emotional connection. It does not need to be a novel experience. It just needs to be the right experience at the best time – and delivered in a way that telegraphs your approach. Approach this as part of a brainstorming user experience exercise, or use your existing application or service but refine the experience. Focus on an activity your customers will experience – building a site, onboarding process, prototype, trial, or campaign. You only focus on one section, page, or component that is pivotal for the customer to experience.

25 minutes

1. Using the UX design components provided (this is a limited list – so feel free to find other resources), divide the workshop into smaller teams of 2-3 people.
2. Ask the teams to answer the question, "**What is the most valued feature or function?**" Give teams 7-10 minutes to do this.
3. Bring the teams together and lead the discussion on the feature/function that is most valued. Allow teams to debate their answers. Facilitate the conversation so that each customer has at least one feature.
    - You can add both features in the box if there is no agreement. Refer to the high and moderate emotions to gain some context. If the facilitation is getting

stuck, either change the feeling or change the feature or function. You are looking for alignment.

- If the group is still undecided, move on to the next exercise to provide some clarification.

20 minutes

4. **Why does it matter to them?"** This is the final step of this exercise. You'll need to ask the participants to address this together.
5. Focus on an alignment across the row. The audience, feature/function, why it matters, and emotions should all make sense to you. You need to aim for agreement among the participants. You should be able to picture it in your mind, to know these customers, and be able to see how the experience could lead to an emotional connection.

Note: *Answers to the question "Why it matters?" should be written in the way the person would say it. Again, the customer-centric perspective matters. What would they say about themselves? What would their internal dialogue be?*

What To Do Next

Now

- This represents a critical finding for elements of your application, site, or campaign that should be shared with internal agencies, marketing teams, and product management to influence their collective understanding of the emotional connection and experience you are creating.
- Make changes or add elements based on input from others outside the workshop group.

Later

- Use this document as the basis for designing specific components. As you plan the various sections of the user experience, keep this front and center. You need to remain focused on your emotional context as you develop the user experiences.

Exercise 5.2: Templates and Examples

- **Figure 34:** Template for the Intersection of Emotional Connection and Digital User Experience (UX) Matrix
- **Figure 35:** Example of the Intersection of Emotional Connection and UX Matrix for Working Dog Site

Figure 34: Template for the Intersection of Emotional Connection and Digital User Experience (UX) Matrix

CUSTOMER	Feature/Function Most Valued	"Why It Matters to Them"	HIGH EMOTION	MODERATE EMOTION	LOW EMOTION
Add Content from Exercise 5.1			Add Content from Exercise 5.1	Add Content from Exercise 5.1	Add Content from Exercise 5.1
Add Content from Exercise 5.1			Add Content from Exercise 5.1	Add Content from Exercise 5.1	Add Content from Exercise 5.1
Add Content from Exercise 5.1			Add Content from Exercise 5.1	Add Content from Exercise 5.1	Add Content from Exercise 5.1
Add Content from Exercise 5.1			Add Content from Exercise 5.1	Add Content from Exercise 5.1	Add Content from Exercise 5.1
Add Content from Exercise 5.1			Add Content from Exercise 5.1	Add Content from Exercise 5.1	Add Content from Exercise 5.1

In this exercise, we have added two columns to the Customer Emotional Connection Template (Figure 32) from Exercise 5.1. The columns are Feature/Function Most Valued and 'Why It Matters to Them" You task is to focus on the emotional digital experience that matches or at least is in alignment to what the customer is feeling.

Figure 35: Example of the Intersection of Emotional Connection and UX Matrix for Working Dog Site

CUSTOMER	Feature/Function Most Valued	"Why It Matters to Them"	HIGH EMOTION	MODERATE EMOTION	LOW EMOTION
Service Dog Trainer	Expert Training Video Library	"I'm following industry standards"	Valued	Successful	Informed
Service Dog Owner (certified)	Certification ID	"I can go everyone I want to go"	Confident	Trusting	Anxious
Therapy Support Dog Trainer	State Rules and Regulations	"I will be in compliance"	Interested	Informed	Capable
Therapy Support Dog Owner	Physician Forms and Process for Medical Clearance	"I know the process"	Overwhelmed	Respected	Informed
Person Verifying Certification of Dog	Registration Database	"I have an official resource"	Empowered	Informed	Curious

The Client Story

When Each Customer Brings Their Unique Emotional Needs

This case is a continuation of the workplace discrimination story from chapter 4. We added the audience's desire for a brand experience that would make them feel better. For each audience strand, there were up to three emotions that were most likely to be desired. The three emotions were ranked from high to low. The statement addressing "Why it matters to them" justified the shift in sentiment. The feature most valued is a digital experience element that would need to be present – alone or with other parts – as evidence that the emotional connection is warranted.

In the case of a person reporting an incident of harassment, the emotional state they are looking for is to feel empowered. Not all reporters want empowerment, but most might feel good about doing something and having a path to help. They may also feel good about being heard, and, given concerns about retaliation, feeling safe is also essential. Some reporters may feel one of these emotions while others have them all.

The "Why does it matter" statement for reporters is "Something is being done. You can imagine if you were in a situation where you witnessed harassment and wanted it to be investigated, stopped, and not repeated. You want something to be done, and if you can report it emotionally, you will probably feel empowered, especially if you can report it in a way that keeps you safe from retaliation. The feature that would go along with this desired emotional state and the "why" is a progress bar or confirmation that an investigation has been started. Progress may simply be pride in having done something. This means you have let a relevant person in authority know there was an incident.

As you scan horizontally, you can see the alignment between what the audience wants to feel, why they want to feel it, and the digital experience. Remember, this exploration happened during the ideation and start-up funding stage. This helped to clarify what would need to be in the working prototype and influenced the development of the minimal viable product (MVP). This exercise – done as part of the messaging strategy – defined the digital experience and product. The emotional shift the various audiences need was built into the experience right from the beginning. So, the customer-centric brand experience is built in from the start.

This exercise and framework also help you see how the audience strands can evolve. Looking vertically, you can see that the statement about "why it matters" is not significantly different across the audience. During any adverse workplace incident, all stakeholders want a similar thing: to know something is being done, control the risk and work on what matters. These are all positive outcomes. For this client, the messaging strategy anchored the narrative around each audience doing the right thing. No matter which audience you were, the right next thing was therefore being done in a way that benefited everyone involved.

Figure 36: Example of the Intersection of Emotional Connection and UX Matrix for Workplace Misconduct Application

CUSTOMER	Feature/Function Most Valued	"Why It Matters to Them"	HIGH EMOTION	MODERATE EMOTION	LOW EMOTION
Reporter / Whistleblower	Progress Bar	"Something is being done"	empowered	heard	safe
CEO	Industry and Culture Index	"I control the Risk"	In control	informed	pride
HR Manager	Process & Steps	"I am working on what matters most to protect the company"	clarity	responsible	responsive
Corporate Lawyer	Alert System	"I know the Risk"	informed		
Board of Directors	Industry and Culture Index	"I control the Risk"	control	informed	pride
Prospective Employees	Index	"They take culture seriously"	informed		

Section 2

Messaging Framework for Digital Engagement

Chapter 6

What Is Your Traditional Messaging Framework?

Key Idea

At this point, you might believe you're ready to create a messaging framework. The previous exercises allowed you to think and see yourself from the customer's perspective. In the workshops, you collaborated with colleagues on the emotional promise and features that would need to be available to trigger emotion-based decision-making.

Traditional messaging frameworks are painstakingly nuanced internal documents created by marketing and strategy experts that provide a high-level communication structure for marketers, agencies, and brand strategists, as well as internal audiences. They serve as an anchor to keep the brand from losing its position. The formats and templates for these communication frameworks solidify agreement – internally across departments and externally – with creative partners.

The framework is a holder of the core messaging strategy; it allows you to see the bones of the brand – either the brand you are or the brand you want to become. Most traditional frameworks include the brand promise, the value proposition, and two or three critical audiences with a bulleted list of key messages for each. Sometimes, brand pillars are added.

At this stage, the framework results from people in the room agreeing on the brand strategy and messaging. However, what if this framework is wrong or our audience isn't ready for such a radical change? Alternatively, the response to this new messaging may be so overwhelming that products, services, and programs would need to change more quickly than they can delivered. For you and your co-creators of the new messaging strategy, do you know what it might look like in the real world?

The traditional messaging framework includes much of what we have covered in the previous chapters. It may be tempting to use the work completed thus far to fill in the messaging framework and be on your way. It would certainly get you further along your path since you have already focused on the customer perspective. If you were to fill this in, you'd do okay if you stayed with the customer's perspective. But okay is just okay. It isn't great. Most marketers and founding teams have difficulty taking the messaging framework and turning it into a digital engagement that reflects the aspects of a brand that matter: the ones that make you uniquely you.

The Traditional Messaging Framework

The traditional messaging architecture gives us a communication structure. It is an important document that requires alignment during the strategic phase. The conventional messaging architecture does two things well:

- Identifying the primary audiences
- Connecting the value of the product or service to that audience

Figure 37: Traditional Messaging Framework

Brand Promise — This is a pledge you make to your customers about what they will experience when they do business with you.

Brand Position — The benefit that sets your brand apart. It is what you want to exist in the minds of your customers. It is your competitive edge.

Value Proposition — A clear statement of the tangible results a customer gets from using your products or services. The more specific the better.

Primary Messages — For each audience there needs to be 3 (usually) primary messages that have to be delivered. The order isn't always as important. Initially, it may be that only one of the messages gets through, but eventually, all messages will be experienced by the audience.

Primary Audience 1 | **Primary Audience 2** | **Primary Audience 3** — Generally there will be two or three roles for Small and Midsize Businesses (SMB). This is the key persona. Yes, there are multiple decision-makers in complex sales, but there will always be a primary.

What Is Wrong with Current Methods?

This doesn't define the emotional relationship or experience, and the connection between the brand and the consumer. This framework, and others like it, is often produced and then stored in a file, never to be reviewed until the brand is in trouble. If it is used, it is by the content marketing team, who usually do a terrific job on the content and messaging strategy from this framework. However, you and others may reject the messaging because you didn't take the same types of messages from this framework. While there is nothing fundamentally wrong with this framework, its problem is that it is not a living, breathing framework that is being referenced or influenced as the brand interacts with customers. There is no bi-directional relationship, no emotion, and no customer perspective.

If I asked you to fill in this framework today (which I will do in the first exercise), you will probably have some ideas and be able to do a decent job. But your initial attempt will not be tested. There will not be a step that verifies whether or not the content you so carefully placed in the framework is sound. You'll need a three-step approach to this framework before it becomes the messaging strategy that will make you great. The first time you fill it in, it will be good. The second attempt will be better, but the third attempt will put you on the path to greatness after you've done the work.

You'll attempt to edit this messaging framework after we have tried to create messaging from it. Think of this as an experimental phase that allows you to translate the framework into an experience that will enable you to see if the framework content is correct. You are checking how aligned you all are. How do you interpret the messaging framework via an in-person, experiential, or digital experience? What would the campaigns, websites, applications, advertising, onboarding, selling, and pricing look like? Without stretching the internal framework to an outward-facing deliverable, there is a risk that you didn't get this exactly right. Skipping this step might mean wasting lots of money, time, and talent rejecting or resisting the messaging that comes from the framework. Suppose you are pivoting your brand, with a temporary revenue loss, and a plan to wean existing clients and introduce a new sales model. In that case, it will be more frightening, chaotic, and potentially so tricky that you retreat to being exactly who you were before.

To combat this, extending the messaging framework to external audiences is helpful. This is to test what this messaging framework might look and feel like. A gut check prevents your organization from throwing everything up in the air and saying, "This isn't working!"

When Do You Need to Address This?

You need to do this anytime your brand is stuck. It might be when you are pivoting to a new audience, introducing a new product or service, or experiencing poor performance on the current marketing approach.

Disappointing Campaign Results

You know there is a problem when campaigns using the new messaging are shut down quickly due to poor performance.

On-boarding Problems

When the onboarding process doesn't match the new promise, as it is not aligned with the new messaging, it confuses potential customers and raises red flags.

Difficulty Getting Approval Of Design

There is also a problem if, when the internal or external creative team is presented with the new messaging, it is heavily edited or downright rejected because it does not "appear" to be "on message." In this scenario, the creative interpretation of the unknown messaging causes so much discomfort that no real change is implemented.

Sales Presentation or Script Not Used

Another warning sign is when changes to the sales presentation or selling script are left untouched by new business development folks who are uncomfortable with pivoting to the new messaging because it is "not working."

Why Doing This Now Will Get You a Better ROI

As part of the creative process, it is easy to react personally to messaging and design, rather than putting yourself in the customer's perspective. It is hard when you must select or approve colors, fonts, copy, and photos that you may not find appealing, but which your audience will respond positively to. If you have the budget to hire a creative agency, you may be presented with concepts that allow you to see different interpretations. But you must still put your feelings aside and test your creative assets to help you remove your own bias and select the option that resonates with your customers. It is also a bigger problem when marketers on a low budget are asked to create materials using SaaS model design platforms. Without design training and skills, the options will be limited to what the marketer can do.

Rather than waste precious time and money interpreting the messaging framework with your initial customers, work on refining it and make sure it is aligned with the eventual customer before it is seen publicly.

How To Fix It - Workshops and Exercises

What Is Your Traditional Messaging Framework?

While you are still in the messaging sessions, stretching the messaging to an audience-facing deliverable will help participants visualize what the new messaging might look like when it is delivered. You want participants to practice what it will be like to encounter the message. The first exercise will focus on filling in the framework. This will be the bulk of the workshop. It is all about selecting the right words that reflect the customer-centric perspective you have established. Often this section of the workshop can feel like it is going off the rails as you move from box to box, realizing how hard it is to "get it right." You don't want to get it right though. You want to get it close.

The second exercise is the cereal box design challenge. This provides an opportunity to translate the internal structure into an external interpretation. This initial exercise is designed to take the pressure off completely. We remove business constraints and dive into the world of a cereal box – the container for a common food item that we are very familiar with. This is about having fun and being creative in an activity with no "right answer." It serves as a vehicle you can use to think about attracting a customer and keeping them interested while they are in a consideration mindset. Because a cereal box is a three-dimensional object and not a web page that can scroll forever, participants need to get an initial message across to gain interest. The limited space also forces the user to place content on different sides – this fosters an intuitive understanding that the user needs to interact with content and be drawn into the messaging.

The third exercise is an improvisation session in which participants to create conversations and dialogue that uses the new messaging in practice. This creative session will allow you to hear what the application of the messages might sound like out loud and within a specific context. Many times, this might be fumbled and imperfect, but it can often unleash a natural, persuasive way to present the new offering.

Exercise 6.1: What Is Your Traditional Messaging Framework?

Timeframe

90 minutes

Focus

Messaging Structure | Design Thinking | Improvisation

Participant Instructions

The traditional messaging framework will change several times. Be ready for it. Give up perfection and embrace the process. You will make incremental changes as you go. The framework will stump you. It is hard to find the right words for what is a critical document that launches ALL YOUR MARKETING. So, the stakes are high. You won't get it right in a single session. Once you and your group get stuck on the framework, creative exercises are introduced to allow you to apply what you are thinking. There is a visual and verbal exercise to accommodate different styles of communication expression. It will feel silly and a bit uncomfortable. Even so, these exercises are designed to help you approach the content that should be included in your messaging using different creative muscles that will reveal more about what you mean and how the messaging might be conveyed to your customers.

Facilitator Instructions

Educationally, this is a working session for which participants must give up the idea of perfection. The grueling and tedious task of building the traditional messaging framework will bring out strong opinions on words and phrases. As it is the first attempt at defining the brand, there will be a resurfacing of old thinking. You can expect one of two reactions: either an attempt to remain vague or an intense desire to be specific. This document will be heavily edited – probably at least five cycles – so this stage is about getting close to what the group believes is the answer. Once you are tight or stuck, move on to one or both of the following exercises. When users need to create an artifact based on the messaging in the cereal box exercise, it helps them to clarify the meaning of it. It opens the discussion to interpreting the current content in the messaging framework. The improv sales presentation is also an excellent sidestep exercise to allow participants who may be more comfortable with verbal expression to try and clarify their take on the messaging framework. You should go back to the messaging framework after exercises 2 and 3 and adjust it accordingly.

Step-by-Step Guidelines

It is helpful for this exercise for individuals to jot down their thoughts first using index cards, post-its, or notebooks. You want to avoid groupthink and encourage a discussion on each component.

15 minutes

1. First, ask each participant to write what they believe is the Brand Promise using their index cards, post-its, or notes. Remember, this is your brand's pledge to your customers about what they will experience when they do business with you.
2. Second, ask participants to identify two or three primary customers. This can be taken from the work in exercises 3.1 or 5.1 and generally narrowed down to two or three

customers for small to mid-sized organizations. This is the critical person. Yes, there are multiple layers of decision-makers in complex sales, but there is always a primary one.

15 minutes

3. Begin trying to create the brand promise from the individuals' input. Start with any participant and have them read their brand promise. Transfer it to the whiteboard or PowerPoint template. Ask participants if they have something similar. As each person shares their promise, begin to create a single promise WITH the participants' help. Once this is close to an agreement, you can move on to the next step.
4. Ask participants to identify the primary customers now. This should be easy if you completed exercises 3.1 or 5.1. Again, this is an excellent moment to ask participants to either make a different choice about whom the brand will target or select the top three customers they chose from the previous exercises.

10 minutes

5. You now need the participants to go back to individual work. With the brand promise and primary customers working on the display, ask for the primary messages for each customer. Each of the three customers will need (usually) two or three primary messages to be delivered during the conversion and engagement process. The order of the three direct messages isn't always as important as the messages themselves. Initially, it may be that only one of

the messages gets through, but eventually, it should all be experienced by the customer. The messaging you add is not the creative interpretation that will eventually be seen on websites and campaigns. This content is for your internal audiences – including all departments and external partners like agencies, and creative firms focused on interpreting your brand.

15 minutes

6. As you did before, have participants share their messages one by one. You'll find some similar notes that quickly collapse into one another. Others will be vastly different. This is a good thing. With your time, get participants to compromise where they can. If they can't, assemble all the messages under each primary customer. This part of the exercise often requires you to move ahead and then circle back to it.

15 minutes

7. You are now ready for the Value Proposition. If you did this exercise as part of chapter 4, you could reintroduce it here. You can lead a discussion to check whether this value statement still feels correct, or whether changes need to be made.
8. If you did not do this exercise in chapter 4, here is a reminder. The Value Proposition clearly states a customer's tangible results from using your products or services. The more specific, the better. This can be done individually, as you did with the other components, or you can try to create this as part of a collaborative exercise.

9. The Value Proposition can take much time to get written. If you have the time, spend it on this statement. But you'll approach this again in the next chapter when we verify if this statement is the same once you come at it from a customer perspective.
10. Use either of the positioning statement formulas in the templates section.

10 minutes

11. Brand Position: The benefit that sets your brand apart is what you want your customers to think. It is your competitive edge. This statement can also benefit participants; have write them down first and share them with the group.
12. As they share, write a single statement on the whiteboard or PowerPoint template.

♥ **Note:** *This one exercise can go on indefinitely. For now, it is just about getting something down that you know you will revisit in the next chapter. Capture the variations and transition to the brand position.*

What To Do Next

Now

- Capture the iterations. As they say, "there is gold in them thar hills!" You can grab or photograph participants' cards.

Later

- The traditional framework is a document you can alter based on what you heard in the workshop and what fits in the messaging hierarchy. Do this on your own or assign a marketing/content strategy person who can help create the messaging framework used in chapter 5.

Exercise 6.1: Templates and Examples

- **Figure 38:** Traditional Messaging Framework Template
- **Figure 39:** Traditional Messaging Architecture Descriptions

Figure 38: Traditional Messaging Framework Template

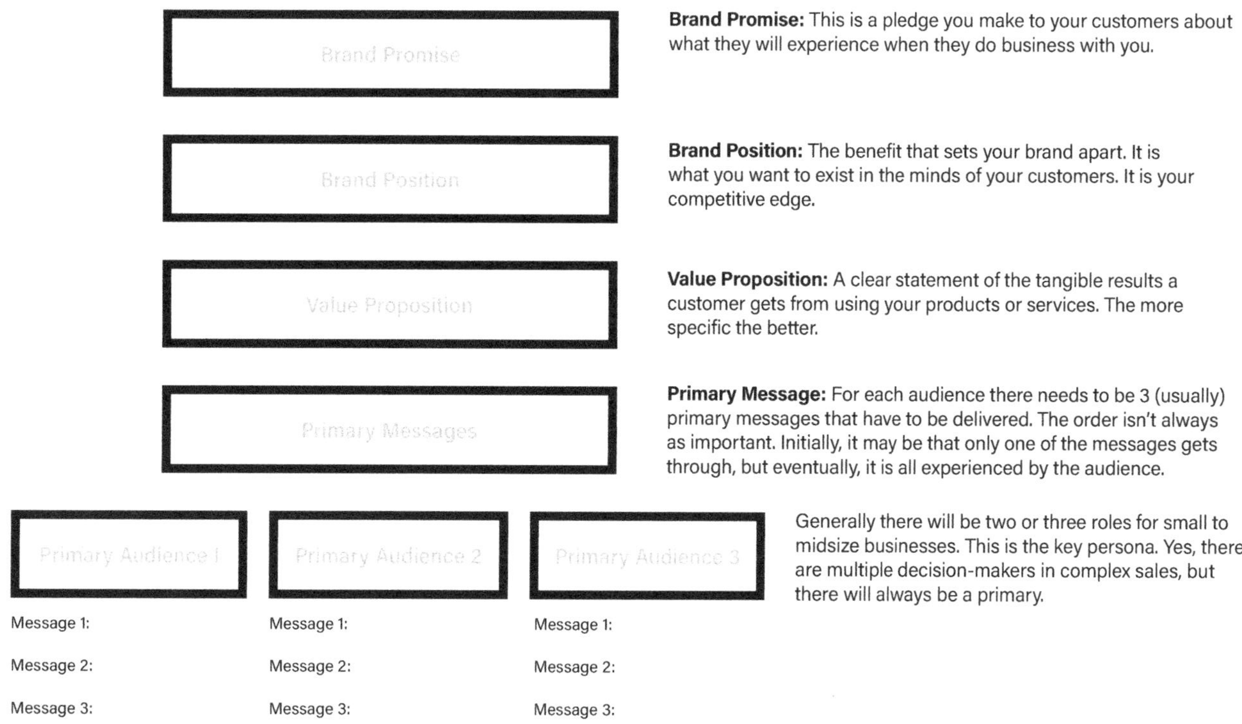

Brand Promise: This is a pledge you make to your customers about what they will experience when they do business with you.

Brand Position: The benefit that sets your brand apart. It is what you want to exist in the minds of your customers. It is your competitive edge.

Value Proposition: A clear statement of the tangible results a customer gets from using your products or services. The more specific the better.

Primary Message: For each audience there needs to be 3 (usually) primary messages that have to be delivered. The order isn't always as important. Initially, it may be that only one of the messages gets through, but eventually, it is all experienced by the audience.

Generally there will be two or three roles for small to midsize businesses. This is the key persona. Yes, there are multiple decision-makers in complex sales, but there will always be a primary.

Figure 39: Traditional Messaging Architecture Descriptions

Brand Promise	This is a pledge you make to your customers about what they will experience when they do business with you.
Brand Position	The benefit that sets your brand apart. It is what you want to exist in the minds of your customers. It is your competitive edge.
Value Proposition	A clear statement of the tangible results a customer gets from using our products or services. The more specific the better.
Primary Audiences 1, 2 and 3	Generally limited to 2 or 3 for a smaller organization, these are the key personas. Yes, there are often multiple decision makers in complex sales, but there is always a primary person.

Exercise 6.2: A Cereal Box (Optional)

Timeframe

30 minutes

Focus

Design Thinking | Creative Interpretation | Content Creation

Participant Instructions

This is an opportunity for you (individually and collectively) to take an initial step toward transitioning from an internal messaging structure to an external expression of the messaging. This will stretch your thinking, as you see the messaging structure being interpreted for the customer. You must work on your own, share your work, and, most importantly, discuss the challenge of communicating the messaging strategy.

Facilitator Instructions

There is often a significant gap between the internal messaging structure and what the creative interpretation will be. In many organizations, internal marketing, UX, content group, or an outside agency make this external creative interpretation. To ensure the messaging is correct, it is helpful for participants to attempt a creative interpretation of their structure to verify if the structure is correct.

This exercise forces participants to see their decisions in a creative interpretation. It will allow you and participants to edit the messaging structure if you find it too tricky or see that it misses the mark when you shift to external messaging. There is great value in asking participants to brainstorm about what they would expect to see, based on their decisions. What is their vision of this messaging structure?

Resources: Exercise 6.2

- Colored pens, magic markers, crayons
- White shipping boxes that are the approximate size of a cereal box

Step-by-Step Guideline

It is important to stress that this is a safe, non-judgmental, creative exercise. This is not about how well you can draw; it is a creative exercise in what you might expect your customers to see.

15 minutes

1. Provide each participant with their shipping box. (If you have a larger group, they can work in teams of 2)
2. Have participants select the customer they want to focus on.
3. Ask your participants:
    - *"If your brand was a cereal box sitting on a shelf with other brands, what would it need to look like to get someone to select it? What is the image, the color, the name, the tagline, the promise – you can take it as far as you need."*
4. Encourage participants to use the front, side panels, and back.

15 minutes

5. Each participant or team should review their design with the group. Keep a positive, encouraging atmosphere as participants share their work – some people can be sensitive about their design skills.
6. You can prompt individuals or conduct a group discussion by asking the following questions.
    - How do the design and content reflect the brand promise?
    - Does the content and design align with one of the messages in the traditional messaging framework?

What To Do Next

Now

- Take photos of the cereal boxes. It is helpful to have a visual reminder of the exercise.
- If the content and design discussion revealed that the participants could not connect the brand promise and message to the cereal boxes, you could capture the dialogue and conversation.
- You could choose to revisit and potentially revise the traditional messaging structure with the participants if the creative work revealed a misalignment.

Later

- If participants don't have the time, you can choose to revisit and potentially revise the traditional messaging structure based on the feedback from this session alone or with a smaller group.

- This exercise often provides a solid foundation for what the creative teams should consider when interpreting the messaging framework. Adding findings from this exercise to a creative brief may be helpful.

Exercise 6.3: Sales Presentation Improv

Timeframe

30 minutes

Focus

Creative Interpretation | Sales Messaging

Participant Instructions

This exercise helps to uncover how the new messaging might be experienced in actual customer interaction. It is not a formal presentation; it is just meant to simulate the type of conversation that may happen. It is an improv exercise, so there is no "right" answer. This is much more about providing people with permission to say whatever comes to mind. Participants are encouraged to be creative and express whatever pops into their heads. Sometimes it will be silly, and other times it may reveal exciting connections, comparisons, and interpretations of how to deliver the messaging.

Facilitator Instructions

You need to set the parameters for an improvisational sales conversation.

There should be no preparing, no overthinking – this is about naturally articulating how a customer and salesperson's discussion might play out. This applies even if, at times, it is silly. The improvisational sales technique will undoubtedly provide humorous moments and reveal exciting positioning in the spontaneous dialogue. It also allows the participants to recognize the difficulty of switching the messaging by actively trying to do it themselves.

This exercise is a demonstration of the new messaging that can, with careful listening, reveal how the sales presentation and campaigns *might* take shape. Observations are key here – allow the participants to experiment with how the messaging could be crafted while recognizing that it will take some trial and error. No perfection. Just play.

Step-by-Step Guidelines

The improv session is followed up with a facilitated discussion on what the experience revealed and whether the new messaging strategy might need an adjustment with respect to the audience, feeling, or features. Also, push one another if the sales discussion feels too generic. This is about connecting to emotional environments, how people feel, and what they want. Generic isn't going to cut it.

15 minutes

1. Depending on the number of participants, you want to divide into teams of two or three. Or you can have two people volunteer to try this exercise in front of the group.
   - If there are only two, one person is the customer, and the other is the salesperson. If there is a team of three, have one person play the customer, and two people play the sales reps.
   - If you don't want or require a salesperson, a good alternative is to substitute the salesperson for a customer support representative or sales development person.
2. It is recommended that you create an actual selling situation that requires you to describe the brand before, after, and in the middle of the sales/onboarding/product assignment.

3. If possible, have three separate teams; each role-plays one of these questions. Team 1 will handle the phase before purchase, Team 2 will address the ongoing process and Team 3 will focus on the follow-up.
4. The focus is on using the new messaging, brand promise, and value proposition in a person-to-person conversation.
5. Set a timer for three minutes. But if the conversation is going well, keep going.
    - Before Purchase
        - It is the final presentation between your brand and a competitor. The customer has asked, *"Why should we choose you?"*
    - The Ongoing Process
        - During the middle of a client project, the relationship between the brand and the customer can be tested. Imagine that you are in that moment when the customer feels particularly vulnerable and wonders if they have made a mistake working with your brand. They are looking for reinforcement of the brand promise. For instance, the person playing the customer might start by saying, "This isn't what I expected it to be like when we signed the contract."
    - Follow-Up
        - Alternatively, imagine you are interviewing a customer who recently completed a project or assignment with your brand. You (the brand) ask the customer, "How would you describe your experience with us?"

15 minutes

6. After the improvs, open the discussion on what felt exciting and compelling about them. This is not a critique but an opportunity to brainstorm on what did seem natural and on point. What would you have liked the customer or salesperson to have been able to say?

What To Do Next

Now

- Take notes (or a record) of the role-playing exercises. You want to capture some of the moments where a frank and compelling discussion embodied the messaging.
- If you have time, repeat the exercise with new teams to see if they can bring something else to the table.

Later

- Transcribe any moments that could be used in the sales training or incorporated into external messaging.
- Also, this content might be helpful; it could end up being reworked as part of the website or advertising content. Questions customers ask before and during projects are excellent content that can be repurposed in blogs, podcasts, landing pages, and demonstrations.

The Client Story

Once You've Seen the Right Path Forward, It Gets Harder To Ignore It

Like many very talented, accomplished, and creative professionals, Irene had developed a successful approach to connecting brands with potential customers by focusing on in-person engagement. The work had helped brands connect in meaningful ways – exceptionally well for purpose-driven markets like clinical trial recruitment. With the idea of building her own business, Irene set out on a messaging strategy exercise to articulate the value creation and unique offering. The work involved seeing herself and her capabilities as a product and service provider as a sole proprietor.

Irene's excellent background and proven track record helped identify audiences and what they valued. Tech CEOs and CMOs were her primary audiences, along with VPs of Clinical Trials. This was an audience Irene had been successful with and could see herself specializing in.

Interestingly, as Irene went through the potential audiences' addressable problems, crisis points, beliefs, how they felt, and what they should feel, the Tech CEOs provoked a slightly different assessment to the other roles.

Figure 40: Example of Customer Empathy Insight Framework The Hurt, Make it Better, Feel Now, and Want to Feel Sections

	CEO Tech Firm	CMO Start Up	Customer Experience Director	Venture Capitalist	Innovation Director	Clinical Trials Director
Emotional Environment	Competitors winning more business	Influencers and prospects can't see the bigger picture.	The decision makers are not involved.	Top talent needs platform to network secretly.	Internal teams frustrated with process and failure.	Obtain enough patients with the tight time frame
Crisis Point	Loyalty and market position is slipping.	Need attention and validation from the right people.	Account-based selling is flat and hard to replicate.	An easier way to secure top talent.	Introduce product/ Service needed to stay in the game.	Reaching the right mix of patients.
Belief	Solidify thought **Leader**ship internally and externally	A **community** can create momentum	**Customers** will tell us what they need from us.	**Top talent** will bring deal flow.	Engage culture and **team** will lead to innovation and profit.	**Patients and their loved ones** use social platforms to find help.
How They Feel Now	Lonely	Pressured	Anxious	Out of Control Frustrated	Overwhelmed	Worried
What They Will Feel	Valued	Successful	Hopeful	Confident	Optimistic	Satisfied

In figure 40 (Potential Audience values and Our Promise to Them), you'll see the CMO (column 2) and Clinical Trial Director (column 6) feeling "pressured' and "worried" respectfully. With Irene, the promise would be that those feelings would change to "successful" and "satisfied". There are similar emotional shifts for all the other audiences except the CEO.

The CEO is lonely, and the emotional value promised is for them to feel valued. There is also a significant difference in the belief system. If you look along the belief row, there are two categories of beliefs. For the CEO and the innovation directions, internal culture and leadership are identified, whereas the audiences are externally focused – on the community, customers, patients, and candidates.

When selecting the primary audiences, the CEO, CMO, and Director of Clinical Trials were prioritized. The brand promise and positioning address external issues – a meaningful connection and engagement with external communities and patients for clinical trials. The idea of "highly curated programs and events that foster meaningful engagement and a (renewed) sense of belonging to a purpose-driven community" reflects the brand's relationship with its external stakeholders. The brand position, to "find the right audience with in-person and digital strategies that authentically connect with people on the vulnerable issues that require care, understanding and personal development" also speaks to identifying customers.

The value proposition, however, is a bit fuzzier. The value proposition speaks to experiences that "change cultures, improve relationships, grow personally and share hope." This value is not necessarily externally facing. This value proposition was crucial for Irene as it tied directly to the CEO as the target audience. The CEO's message speaks to internal issues like "confidentially creating a custom program to fix core problems, identify the vulnerable matters, and develop trust and a healing culture." In this traditional messaging framework, we see a result of a brand making a messaging strategy with two very different strands. The traditional messaging framework did not prevent the selection of two different directions because it was built from the brand's perspective. It reflected the fact that the brand did not do what the customers needed most from the brand. Interestingly, this exercise highlighted the tension between two very different potential directions for the brand. It reflected two possible companies, not one unified brand.

Figure 41: Example of Messaging Framework for Marketing Consultant

Brand Promise (customer experience) Custom programs that create opportunities for meaningful engagement and sense of belonging in a purpose-driven business.
Brand Position (benefit that sets you apart) Identify and reach the right people and build authentic, caring connection and commitment to personal development
Value Proposition (tangible customer benefit) Insights and experiences that move people to improve relationships and change culture

Target Audiences

CEO

- Build a culture that fuels growth of employees
- Find advisors and experts to guide my personal growth
- Develop leadership team that believes in a culture based on trust

CMO

- Reach new audiences
- Create impactful customer experiences
- Build a community with true connections

Clinical Director

- Directly connect with patients and caregivers
- Easier online self-selection and onboarding process for client trial consideration
- Provide hope for vulnerable people who have limited options

Irene was committed to creating a viable company. She built a website and began to market the brand to the CMOs and VPs of clinical trials. As the initial prospects started to ask questions, Irene still had two potential directions. She soon realized that the work she was most passionate about was the value proposition and messaging related to the CEO. Irene wanted to help change the culture by working directly with leaders on their skills. Having gone through the messaging strategy helped highlight this conflict and opened the door to working with CEOs and leaders. And it helped Irene pivot to the business she most wanted to build.

Chapter 7

What Is Your Customer-Centric Messaging Framework?

Key Idea

Training ourselves to consider the customer perspective is a new and challenging mindset. As marketers, you constantly switch views to see the problems and solutions from every angle. As you shift from the brand viewpoint to the customer's perspective, it's easy to slip into old thinking that sabotages your efforts. The current frameworks we use to help us create messaging and content do not prevent us from falling into brand-centric thinking. The traditional messaging strategy framework was constructed long before the idea of customer-centricity would be incorporated into digital experiences and transformation. It's based on your perception (and your team's perception) of what customers want; this creates an inability to get to the core customer-first approach. Since the message strategy framework is the first of many marketing documents, it can set you up for messaging that will not truly connect with customers.

If you have completed the traditional messaging strategy, you might move on to begin developing all the additional marketing documents required to create brand engagement. But what if you didn't get this first document right? The cascading documents will all be wrong. Then, what is wrong in the initial messaging will be compounded in everything you create. Getting it right is essential if the entire digital experience flows from the messaging strategy. Testing that you have it right is vital.

What Is Wrong with Current Methods?

Traditional marketing materials scatter valuable information across many documents, providing a sliver of customer insight. Depending on how sophisticated your marketing is, you may have some, all, or none of these documents. Generally, they are created separately from one another, don't always include the same internal and external teams, and are rarely updated or referenced – unless there is a problem.

Additionally, the documents are not connected to a single over-arching customer-centric document. These documents do provide some value, but only if they are built on the customer-centric approach from the start.

If, for example, your initial value proposition is not connected to the best audience, the personas you target will not be correct. If your customer journeys and empathy maps do not consider how your customers currently feel and would like to feel, then you risk not being able to connect or engage with the customers who truly want you.

Look at this grid of brand documents containing a piece of the customer-centric experience. You can see that their culmination should provide a solid connection to the customer and their brand experience. It SHOULD all be there. And yet, your brand may not be meeting your revenue targets. So, where do you start to fix the problem?

Figure 42: Customer Information and Insights Spread Across Many Documents

<table>
<tr><th>Brand Documents</th><th>What It May Contain</th></tr>
<tr><td>Traditional Messaging Strategy Framework</td><td>Brand Promise | Brand Positioning | Value Proposition | Primary Audiences | Primary Messaging</td></tr>
<tr><td>Personas</td><td>Attributes | Attitudes | Needs</td></tr>
<tr><td>Empathy Maps</td><td>Thinking | Hearing | Seeing | Saying</td></tr>
<tr><td>Customer Journeys</td><td>Connections | Interactions | Moments of Truth</td></tr>
<tr><td>Perception Maps</td><td>Competitive Positioning | Gaps in Market</td></tr>
<tr><td>Customer Insights</td><td>Market Research | Focus Groups | Third Party Customer Data</td></tr>
<tr><td>UX / UI Testing and Workshops</td><td>Data Collected | Sales Funnel | Engagement Problems</td></tr>
<tr><td>Industry Reports</td><td>Market Trends | Benchmarks | Playbooks | Best Practices | Case Studies</td></tr>
<tr><td>Social Media Listening</td><td>Monitor | Respond | Analyze Social Conversation</td></tr>
<tr><td>Content Strategy</td><td>Tone | Voice | Information</td></tr>
<tr><td>Information map</td><td>Information Hierarchy | Navigation mapping</td></tr>
</table>

Part of adopting a customer-centric messaging approach is ensuring the documents you depend on are accurate. Is the customer represented? Did you define the customer's perspective during workshops, discussions, conversations, and communications about the messaging strategy? I have noticed in many sessions that those representing the brand speak about their view of the customer but cannot remain neutral. Here is an example of all the documents that flow from the traditional messaging strategy framework. How you interpret customer insight and industry reports, select personas, and empathize with them are all affected by the initial perspective. The digital experience that follows cascades from there – allowing things that are not entirely correct in the beginning to be pulled into every aspect of the brand experience. This is why you experience problems down the line but cannot fix them – because the essential- messaging framework is flawed.

To be customer-centric, you must "invite" the customer's perspective into all dialogue. This isn't about polling, focus groups, or listening campaigns – though they are valid and should be part of what you consider. What you need to do today is invite the customer into the room by flipping the conversation entirely. You need to reverse the messaging strategy framework to see what your messaging strategy would be like if your customer's perspective were the leading voice. What if we built our messaging strategy framework with a flipped approach? This is an excellent time to test how aligned you are with what customers want. Suppose you made it from the customer's perspective. Would the brand promise be the same?

A new customer-centric messaging framework will help solidify the brand experience. It will align more with customers' emotional needs, desires, and user experiences. All the subsequent documents cascading off them would be far more accurate. Any glitches in the shift to old ways of thinking could have some chance of being caught during the process. The chances of delivering a significantly better customer experience would also increase if everything from our messaging framework to our digital expertise were aligned. A new framework must be introduced because our old framework was never built for a high level of customer-centricity and the competitive advantage of a digital experience.

Look at the slight difference between the traditional messaging framework and the customer-centric framework. In the conventional framework, you start with the brand promise and positioning. Each step trickles down to the next piece, influencing the content until we finally get to the customers at the end. The order affects both the customer experience and the messaging. Additionally, we include products, services, and benefits in the previous steps and don't have much consideration for emotional needs, connections, or digital experience. If we genuinely embrace customer-centricity, we must lead with the customer.

In the customer-centric messaging framework, the primary audiences, along with their emotional connections and needs, lead the process. It is the customers who influence all the other strategic messaging.

Changes to the Primary Customer and Messaging

We ingrain the customer in the emotional connection we need to establish and the needs we address. The customer is represented as a thinking, feeling person with a need. And the preliminary messaging reflects that need. It keeps it highly focused on what your brand needs to be to a genuine person and other people like them.

Changes to the Value Proposition

The value proposition thus shifts from "tangible results" to both tangible and intangible value. We elevate the idea of what a customer **gets** from using a product or service to what the customer **gets from experiencing** the product or service. The value proposition is secondary because it should directly reflect the customers, what value they will get, and their experiences of you – not just in the purchase and use of your products and services but in all interactions.

Changes to the Brand Position

The brand position is still about the benefit that sets you apart. What is different is the enhancement of what you are in the minds and hearts of your customers. Becoming relevant requires you to act like close friend to your customer. This creates is a stronger bond and a clear line between your relationship and what they feel when they consider other brands.

Changes to the Brand Promise

This definition requires only one small change. Traditionally, we talk about what happens "when customers do business with you." I switch this to what happens "when customers interact with you." Not everything in business should feel like business, especially when they are like close friends. And you must compete on their experience of the brand. So, you are promising them an experience.

Figure 43: Updating Descriptions to Incorporate Customer Centricity

	Old Definition	Updated Definition
Brand Promise	This is a pledge you make to your customers about what they will experience when they do business with you.	No change.
Brand Position	The benefit that sets your brand apart. It is what you want to exist in the minds of your customers. It is your competitive edge.	The benefit that sets your brand apart. It is what you want to exist in the minds **and hearts** of your customers. It is your competitive edge **and relevance**.
Value Proposition	A clear statement of the tangible results a customer gets from using our products or services. The more specific the better.	A clear statement of the tangible **and intangible value** a customer gets from **experiencing** our products or services. The more specific the better.
Primary Audiences 1, 2 and 3	Generally limited to 2 or 3 for a smaller organization, these are the key personas. Yes, there are often multiple decision makers in complex sales, but there is always a primary person.	**Three Emotion + Need Message Statements for Each Customer**
Brand Experience	*Not considered in the old definition.*	**Universal customer experiences that build affinity, alignment, and attachment.**

When Do You Need to Address This?

You know you need this if you have only done a more traditional framework or basic brand strategy and are still fuzzy about your messaging. There may be frustration and confusion within the organization regarding the brand strategy and messaging, causing endless conversations and cycles with no resolution. You could be at the beginning stage of a product launch or wondering why your customer experience – online or offline – isn't jiving. It is also useful when you wonder if you should pivot to a different model and offering.

New Brand Launch

When you are launching a new product or brand, many shortcuts will be taken in the quest just to get something to market. This exercise will help you be honest in your customer-centric approach and ensure the initial launch is aligned with the beta customers.

Brand Strategy Failure/Pivot

If the initial launch has been unsuccessful, it may be hard to discern where the mistake was. Is the product or service genuinely wrong? Was it the audience? The positioning? The marketing campaigns? Tensions will be running high, with lots of blame going around, but no one is sure exactly what caused the failure. This exercise can help in that scenario.

Current Messaging Not Working

Do you find that customers who are interested in your products or services are surprised at the pricing, process, length of time it takes, and steps required to receive the products or services? This is less about not attracting customers at all – which would mean that you need to start at chapter 1 – this is about being off target enough that it is hurting but could be fixed.

Why Doing This Now Will Get You a Better ROI

If you and your friend make a promise to one another, but one of you does not fulfill that promise as expected, uneasiness can develop into distrust. Your customers are choosing to engage with you. They are looking for evidence that they can feel secure with you. It can only be true if the experiences match it. Customers want to know they are making good decisions – even in the early stages of research and consideration. They are also interested in feeling good about the process and gaining a sense of progress – both on the decision and the compilation of the evidence that you are a brand they can trust. The experience of the brand must be an extension of the messaging strategy. The promise you make should be experienced throughout the engagement.

Many start-ups and early-stage firms never made it out of the gate because they did not understand who their customer was and what they wanted. Many brands reach a certain revenue number and never seem to be able to exceed it. These are often the results of messaging made from the brand's perspective.

How To Fix It - Workshops And Exercises

Can You Make a Holistic Shift from a Traditional to a Customer-Centric Framework?

The Customer-Centric Messaging Framework™ is a compilation of much of the work done in the previous chapters. This exercise allows you to rebuild your messaging based on previous insights and experiences, and to shift the organization to a customer's perspective. This workshop will draw on the earlier findings and wisdom, but when assembled, it can still be refined to reflect your differentiation and path to emotional connection based on shared values.

Exercise 7.1: What Does *Your* Customer-Centric Messaging Framework Look Like?

Timeframe

60 minutes

Focus

Messaging Structure | Messaging Strategy

Participant Instructions

Suppose you have just completed the traditional messaging framework. This exercise may be more complicated if you cannot give up some of your thinking during the earlier activities. Changing your perspective gives you a new lens from which to see things. If you try to edit the items just slightly to speed through this, you will be doing yourself and your brand a disservice.

Haste leads to disaster. An inability to make changes will prevent you from having a deep, engaging relationship with customers.

Facilitator Instructions

In this exercise, we compile the previous work to assemble a customer-centric messaging framework. This can be approached in two ways.

Approach 1

You can use the traditional messaging framework and rework it based on the content, ideas, and decisions made in previous chapters. You will transfer the standard framework content to this customer-centric framework and begin an editing process that shifts the perspective. This will be heavily influenced by decisions made during the process outlined in this book. You or a small team can do this and review in a collaborative discussion format where input and feedback are encouraged.

Approach 2

You can work with a small cross-functional team to build the customer-centric framework without using the traditional messaging framework as a resource. This approach would systematically assemble the framework from previous chapters to build the strategy from scratch. This is a collaborative discussion format, where input and feedback are encouraged, and final decisions are made.

Step-by-Step Guideline

30 minutes

1. You will be selecting two or three audiences. For each audience, compile the work you already did in previous exercises.
2. This is a restructuring of the primary target audience, based on connecting emotions and values from customers' perspectives.
3. It may be helpful to use a larger version of the circles to see how you are building the diagram from the inside out.

Figure 44: Customer-Centric Messaging Framework™ Diagram

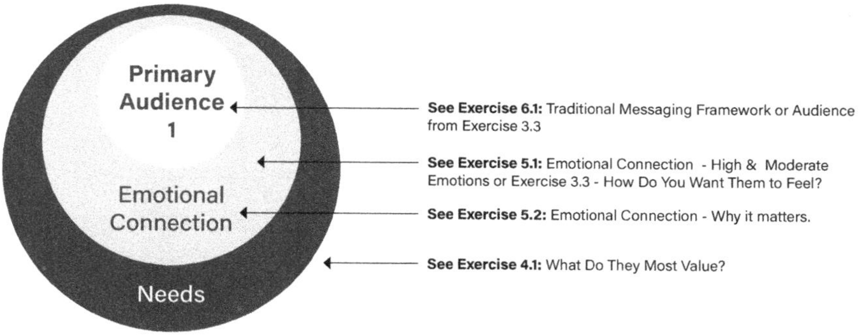

- Emotion + Need Message A
- Emotion + Need Message B
- Emotion + Need Message C

4. You want to repeat this process for the two or three audiences you are working on. If possible, try not to make edits at this stage, just pull in the content and review for accuracy and cohesiveness.

10 minutes

5. Once you have compiled all three as a group, ask yourself, "Do you know this person?" and "Is this the customer who needs us?"
   - At this phase, remember that the messages are internal. They are the baseline for more refined messaging AND a digital experience and the messaging framework. Resist deep editing at this stage. Keep building.

20-30 minutes

6. Pull in that content for this exercise if you built the traditional messaging framework. If you did not, facilitate a draft of the following statements from above.
7. **Value Proposition:** A clear statement of the **tangible and intangible value** a customer gets from **experiencing** your products or services. The more specific, the better.
8. **Brand Position:** The benefit that sets you apart. It is what you want to exist in the **minds and hearts** of your customers. It is your competitive edge **and your relevance.**
9. **Brand promise:** The pledge you make to your customers about what they will experience when interacting with you.
10. **Brand experience: The universal customer experiences that build affinity, alignment, and attachment.**

What To Do Next

Now

- Managing the crafting of these statements might get a little messy – especially if there is input from a lot of people. Capture what you have so it can be compiled into a clean version.

Later

- A smaller group should work on a final version of this framework. It is helpful to circulate it one more time for final comments.
- Watch for the brand's perspective creeping back.

Exercise 7.1: Examples And Templates

- **Figure 45:** Example from the Workplace Misconduct Application
- **Figure 46:** Customer-Centric Messaging Framework™ Template

Figure 45: Example from the Workplace Misconduct Application

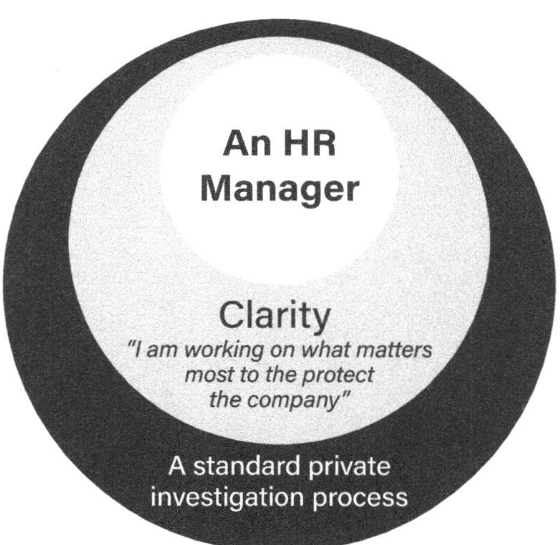

- Clarity - I need to know what to do
- Responsible + I can protect the company
- Responsive + I am working on the most important cases

Figure 46: Customer-Centric Messaging Framework™ Template

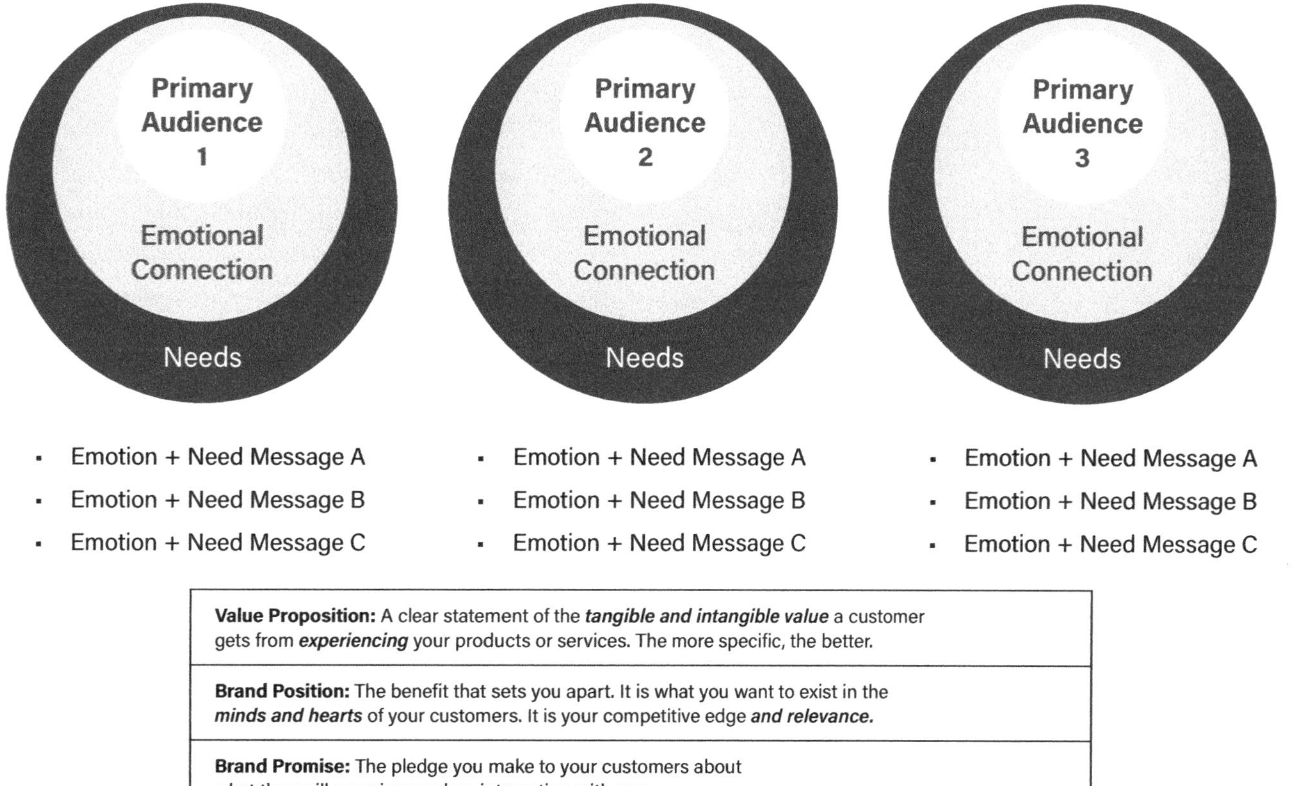

Value Proposition: A clear statement of the ***tangible and intangible value*** a customer gets from ***experiencing*** your products or services. The more specific, the better.
Brand Position: The benefit that sets you apart. It is what you want to exist in the ***minds and hearts*** of your customers. It is your competitive edge ***and relevance.***
Brand Promise: The pledge you make to your customers about what they will experience when interacting with you.
Brand experience: ***The universal customer experiences that build affinity, alignment, and attachment.***

A Client Story

Creating a Digital Experience Based on True Empathy and Emotional Understanding

In all my years of messaging, I have had a few clients who genuinely do know their customers. One such client is Sasha, an exceptionally successful tech entrepreneur who reinvented themselves into a best-selling author, speaker, thought leader, and advocate for healing from burnout. Sasha had always had a keen understanding of her customers. She connects well with people – she has a charismatic personality, and is very smart, aware, and knowledgeable about the connection between messaging and brand experience.

Sasha was aware that she was the brand. As a speaker, workshop leader, and consultant, her own story, transformation, and transcendence served as an example. While we all have a personal brand, for some businesses, a decision needs to be made about the person (CEO, Founder, Talent, or Inventor) who represents the brand. Customers want a relationship with the person – even if it isn't a personal connection – it needs to feel like you "know" them. The customers can self-select to be loyal friends, familiar acquaintances, or die-hard fans. In this case, the brand was Sasha, and Sasha was the brand. And the customers would require messaging to connect with her on what felt like a personal level.

When I was working with Sasha, she had exceptional data from her followers. She had captured usability data, conducted focus groups, and built relationships with highly loyal customers who showed signs of wanting to become influencers – sharing their experiences of recovering from burnout. During the messaging sessions, we started with the existing customers' experience of Sasha and her products and services, and the way they wanted to interact with and become even more involved with the brand. From the beginning, the messaging framework started with the customer's perspective. There was great material on customers' and prospects' emotions and what they wanted to feel. The messaging framework was built on the messaging needed for new and current customers who desired a friend who had been through what they were going through and could show them that they could feel a new emotion.

In essence, in this business model, you are creating a celebrity version of yourself. This model will ensure success in many speaking, consulting, thought leadership, and publishing realms. Building your messaging strategy on customers' relationships with the celebrity version of you becomes crucial. And this means a messaging strategy that starts with what your customers want – this must be a path to get closer to you (theoretically) via the digital experience and interactions.

An exciting part of this messaging experience with Sasha was the ability to list the experiences and interactions customers would want and how those interactions would result in customers feeling closer to the Sasha brand. The messaging and the interactions that would lead to a relationship were how the messaging frameworks were built. The brand promise, position, and value proposition came last. I still remember how easy it was to draft the brand promise, position, and value proposition because Sasha knew what the customers needed and how she would provide it via her brand experience.

Starting with the customer messaging allowed Sasha to launch a personal brand that immediately resonated with current and new customers who identified directly with the messaging and had a digital path through which to begin feeling better via the tools and a feeling of connection with a trusted friend who could help.

Chapter 8

Will Customers Listen?

Key Idea

As marketers, you have many tools that capture the tiny sliver of your customer's life that concerns you. There are personas, empathy maps, customer insight reports, market research, focus group findings, industry reports, competitive analysis, and the customer journey diagram.

And still, you have difficulty identifying exactly what to say. How do you connect in a way that allows you to reach people with messaging they will listen to? How do you select what's important from so much data and insight?

The customer-centric messaging approach is a framework that has helped you see the customer's perspective. But the messaging framework and digital experience you envisioned need to be presented to the customers in a way that they will listen to. Forget brand speak for a minute and shift to person-to-person communication. Let's say your friend is upset about a situation and is thinking about doing something rash – like sending a scathing email to their boss. If you want to convince a friend to consider other options, the first thing you'll do is listen to them vent. You will acknowledge how they feel, repeating back to them the words and evidence they have shared. The first order of marketing is much the same. You need to show you are listening. You understand their current position and thought process.

As you acknowledge perspective, you start to create a bridge between the actions your friend is currently considering and introduce alternative responses. The same is true for customer-centric messaging. It would help if you acknowledged what the customers are now feeling—to hear what they are dealing with—as you seek an opening for introducing an alternative. You need to, in some respects, mirror what they are saying so they know that you understand their problems. But you need to do so in a way that allows you to position your messaging as a unique solution from someone who understands. You grab them by showing you hear them. You hold on to them by acknowledging that their current alternative will relieve some pain. But you embrace them when you offer a solution that will be far better than what they are currently planning or have. As a customer moves through the decision-making process, their perspective shifts. Messaging must shape that perspective in your favor. Your messaging must feel relevant to their current viewpoint and begin to change how they view, consider, and pursue their alternatives in a way this is most aligned with your brand's viewpoint.

The words we use matter. A precise choice of words sends a signal to our customers. How we describe products and services can be deep and profound, or we can use complex terms, details, technical jargon, or words that stay on the surface. It is also important to consider the role of gender in vocabular choice. In one study of venture capital presentations, researchers wanted to understand why female entrepreneurs were not being funded at the same rate as male entrepreneurs. The study found that female entrepreneurs discussed their business using more complex vocabulary and had highly detailed plans for product innovation, go-to-market strategy, and how the funds would be utilized. On the other hand, males did not provide details, spoke in general words, and lacked the level of detail to prove they had a well-thought-out plan. The predominantly male venture capitalist believed the male entrepreneurs would be more successful, not because of evidence of the business plan but because the vocabulary matched their communication style.

What Is Wrong with Current Methods?

For your customers to accept your messaging, they need to hear it in a way that matches how they communicate. Your customer is trying to connect the content, opinions, advice, recommendations, information, and experiences from many sources of communication. Your responsibility is to help them make sense of the content between the different sources and to see that your product or service is connected to their wants and needs. Depending on the industry, messaging may be through analyst reports, white papers, playbooks, case studies, and guidebooks. Marketing campaigns, thought leadership initiatives, and product reviews created by you and competitors can be overwhelming. All the various, often conflicting content and lack of any distinguishable differentiation, leave potential customers feeling that brands don't understands them. This is the background against which you and your competitors are fighting to get into the discussion, thought process, and consideration set.

Figure 47: The Messaging Landscape

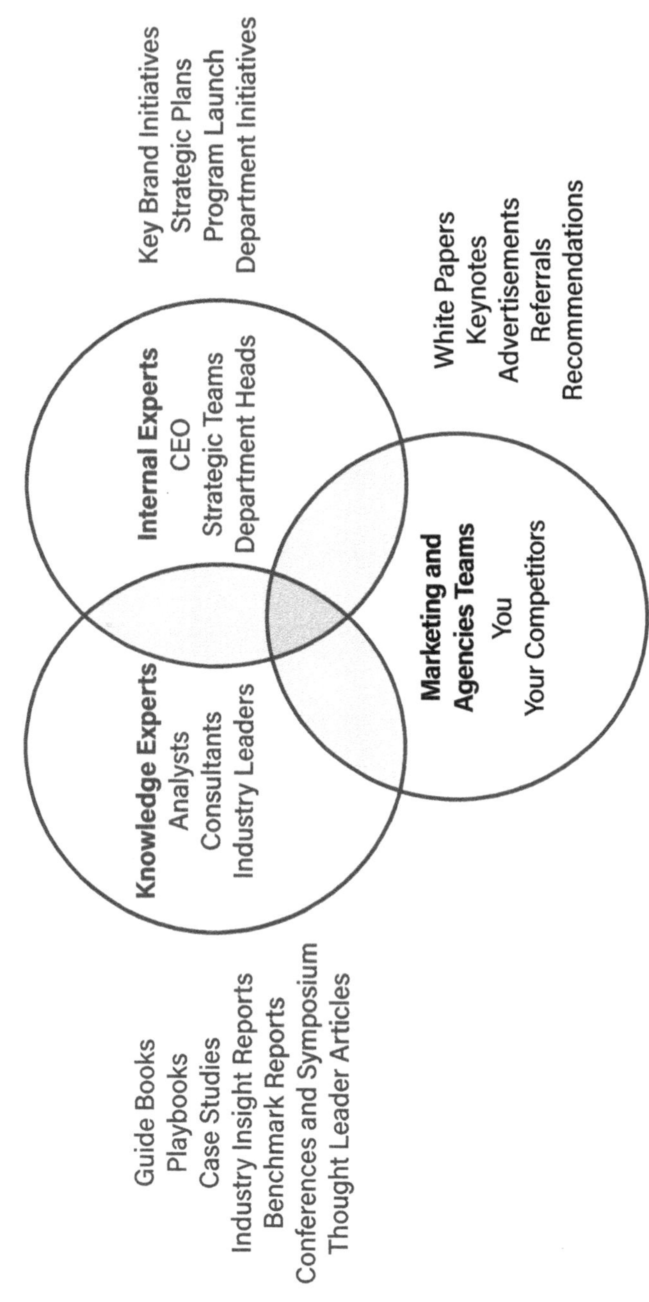

Figure 47 is a diagram of the different types of messaging that your customers are trying to reconcile and synthesize to gain some momentum. While you may have a new and different approach, there needs to be some content that links what they are hearing to what they need to consider. An essential missed step is identifying the gap between how you see the problem and how the customer is experiencing the problem. Customers are experiencing many messages that they are trying to categorize into two main buckets that eventually will lead them to their selection. Bucket one is 'this sounds like me' and bucket two is 'this isn't for me.' Your messaging, content, and digital experience needs to build a bridge from where the customer currently is (their experience of the problem) to what is could be (their experience of the solution). To build the bridge you need to help make sense of all the messages for the potential customer. It's important to start with a theme analysis. What are the narrative themes your customers are experiencing? If you were to evaluate all the content they can access, what will they believe is the path forward? How will you help them make sense of it all? How can you get them to cross your bridge.

How To Fix It - Workshops and Exercises

Narrative And Theme Analysis

To build a messaging strategy must include an evaluation of the current messages influencing your customer. It is helpful to review as much of this content as you can. There will be some reports – especially analysts or industry reports that are only available for a fee. However, there is usually enough information available to gather the key themes and talking points for free..

This exercise focuses on how your industry is talked about by the thought leaders, influencers, and experts who weigh in on high-level issues and define the framework from which your prospective customers view their own problems. With a focus on your customer, you need to look at the messaging being marketed to them.

Even if, let's say, your customer is a mid-level manager, how are they being managed and directed to solve problems from the senior teams or c-suite. It's important to understand how your customer's company is being influenced. What are the members of the board of directors, c-suite, senior team, and stakeholders reading, listening to, and discussing? And how will your customer – the mid-level manager – need to solve the problem based on what they are being told and how they are being told to resolve it?

Figure 48: Consumer-Centric Messaging Insight Research Framework™

	Industry Reports, Articles, and Podcasts	White Papers	Case Studies	Keynote and Thought Leadership Messages	RFPs, SOWs and Customer Inquiries
Content themes from past two years	Common themes you see across the board. Usually presented from different angles but saying about the same thing.	Review for common problems faced by your target audience. Are their differences in the key points being raised?	What do competitors say about the criteria for getting the initial engagement?	Review the keynote and featured speaker titles and bullet points. What is the content theme?	What you are being asked to do? What are the questions you face during the sales process?
Similar themes across competing organizations	What are similar themes you see from direct and indirect competitors?	What are the similarities in competitive approaches to the problems?	Is there REALLY a difference in how they describe the problem, the process they use, and the results?	What are the commonalities at the most popular talks at the biggest conferences?	What are customers asking for or going to others to fulfill work you do?
Future considerations	When they provide advice, it is short term, long term, or actionable? Do they mention the scenarios that represent time for action?	What are the themes described across the white papers that tell the customer what to look for when it is time to act?	What are the issues that mentioned in next steps?	Are there people talking about new approaches and innovative ideas that seem impossible or too far reaching?	What long-term initiative are you seeing from start ups or futurist who are shaping changes in the industry?
Next steps and timelines	What are your prospective customers being advised to do and when?				
Resistance	What are the themes of resistance for this content?				

This Messaging Insight Research Framework™ summarizes significant themes that influence prospective and existing customers thinking, feeling, actions, and experience. By looking at the industry and competitors from the customer's perspective and mapping where and by whom they are influenced—you can fully appreciate how the content shape decisions. You'll see how the internal client dialogue leads directly to how people search for solutions, what words they use, who they consider, what content they seek. You'll also see weaknesses in your competitor's messaging that you can take advantage of. By seeing the industry from your customer's lens, you can create messaging that is exactly what they are looking for. And, in turn, see how the customer will evaluate and implement solution.

In essence, you build trust with the people you are designing your products and services for by embracing their worldview and introducing them to yours. You gain understanding – true understanding being alignment between sender and receiver. Being understood is disruptive. Simple, clear messaging takes a lot of effort – but it is the right and most rewarding place to focus your energy.

The Client Story

Would You Give Up Your Best Customer for a Scalable Model?

I was once brought in as CMO of a start-up eCommerce company. The technology had been built by a few guys who had successfully attracted some initial customers. Venture capitalists could see a good thing coming and put in funds and a new management team to grow the firm. The eight-person start-up with people in Spain, Boston, New York, Canada, and Atlanta quickly became 25 people charged with scaling fast. My job was to find the position, define the promise, generate leads, and put the firm in a leadership position in about six months. (This is the typical request of a tech start-up CMO and, while it is entirely ridiculous, we always say 'sure!'). This was early in the eCommerce technology SaaS space, where retailers needed ways to manage online purchases and fulfillment. At this stage, the technology to help retailers create online shopping didn't have a pricing model. With heavy time and money investment in building an online store that augmented the brick-and-mortar store, the firms providing the technology and the retailers had to create a way to make it profitable while navigating the disruptive stage of shopping as we knew it.

As the CMO, I had to define a brand direction when the existing customers had different needs. On one end, there were luxury clients– who sold very few items online since most customers used the site to window shop, then went to the store to try on and purchase. Then there were fully online brands that needed a sophisticated order management system to stay profitable. Founders, C-suites, client services, sales development, and customers each wanted something different. Our roadmap needed to match with the customers who would make us profitable. That meant we needed to say no to some customers – the low volume luxury brands of the world. However, getting a start-up to give up its marquee client would not be easy.

Part of the problem was defining what the SaaS model pricing would be based on. Was there a fee for every transaction, a monthly fee for the platform, or a bundled approach with a price for the base product with the ability to add new features for additional costs? Acceptance of or resistance to the business and pricing model depended a great deal on the size of the retailer and their viewpoint of how eCommerce would affect their business. Retailers who believed their customers would want to shop online but make the final purchase in person felt very differently about the pricing than the purely online retailers.

To help articulate the messaging strategy and connect with the best type of retailer required a narrative that helped alleviate the stress and anxiety of businesses in the throes of industry disruption. For many potential customers, there was a fear that selecting the wrong technology would put them out of business. For many, their dreams and livelihood were on the line. Passionate founders, demanding investors, and a well-intentioned C-suite looking for alignment and traction added to the chaos being felt by the customers and prospects.

The only way to move forward was to see the online retailing world from the customer's point of view. What were they being told by their customers, what did they hear at conferences, and how fast was online consumer shopping being adopted according to the experts and analysts? Were shipping and returns eating away at profits? If so, when would the shipping companies start to offer standard rates and better turnaround times that could improve levels of cart abandonment?

The consumer insight and analysis painstakingly painted a picture where the purely online retailers with significant inventory were the businesses that had a do-or-die decision to adopt order management systems that could create efficiencies and provide end-to-end tracking. By homing in on the retailers who stood to benefit the most and had no real option but to adjust to the changing dynamics of the industry, a particular type of retailer we should focus on emerged. And we learned to speak with them from their perspective. We sought to understand their world and show them what could be with our SaaS technology.

Interestingly, the exercise also helped the product development, sales, and C-suite to know precisely how critical it was to have a technology for retailers doing over $2 million worth of business with more than 100 SKUs and shipping nationwide. This was the perfect customer. After that, a pricing decision and product direction could be made from the customer's perspective. Addressing the emotional environment of overwhelmed retailers losing margin when their customers purchased the wrong product helped the company focus on the pressure retailers faced and their customers' anxiety.

Chapter 9

Becoming a Brand Customers Love

Becoming a customer-centric brand is extremely difficult. It takes deep effort to listen to customers. To find or create a market, you need to see the potential customers who would love your brand. Part of the problem is timing. Marketing used to be the fast food of business function: yielding quick results, speedy service, and open 24-7. However, that isn't a path to healthy relationships with customers who want meaningful connections with brands.

So far, you have used the workshops and exercises in this book to define all the components of a messaging strategy. You have collaborated and debated about who your actual customers are, what they want from you, and how they feel before, during, and after engaging with your brand experience. You also developed new ideas of how to position and talk about what you are offering.

At this point, it may feel like you have fragmented answers. However, you have already completed a feat that many failed and struggling businesses never do – you have begun the process of leading your organization into deep, caring engagements. You have shifted the viewpoint of the product teams, senior management, sales, marketing, content marketing, user experience teams, and agencies to that of the customer. And you have gained a new role and skills as the leader of the customer-centric strategy. You are becoming a living brand responding to values and emotional needs. You are ready to develop digital engagement that communicates your understanding.

Now, the discussion of customer-centricity can be replaced with action and processes that flip the way we approach brand strategy, digital engagement, and experience. By moving the messaging to the beginning – and shifting to the customer's perspective as you do so, you will align your brand value with the one element that is vital to your success: namely, your customers. And not just any customer. The ones who love you.

Acknowledgements

This book is a dream come true and it took the support and love of many to become a reality. My children, Liza, Ruby, and Ella were my biggest fans. Thank you for giving me the time I needed to write and for your insightful input along the way. And to Talulah – who provided the emotional support that only a sweet chocolate lab can provide.

I'd like to thank my favorite sister, Kathy who always has time to listen to my rants. My brother-in-law, Wayne, was the first person to tell me I had a way with words – and since he is a fantastic human, I believed him. I do not know what I would do without my brother, Skip – who has given me so much. And much appreciation to my other favorite sister, Karen Ann. I am so lucky for my small, mighty family – Christine, Charlotte, Griffin, Russell, Tammy, Jimmy, Terry, Jason, and Eric. I love you all.

To my extremely talented RedSwan5 colleagues Michelle Archambault and Patti Morsillo who held the fort down while I wrote this book – I could not have done this without you. And to the people who keep me from getting lost, my wonderful friends Sarah Cardozo Duncan, Izzy Gesell, Matthias Ehrhardt,

Maren Rossman, Beazie Chase, Pat Hambrick, Arafat Kazi, Denice Sakakenny, and Miriam and James Alandydy.

The actual writing of this book happened at Writing in Community (WIC) - a group led by Kristin Hatcher. I owe a lifetime of gratitude to Regina Ochoa, Joyce Sullivan, Chad Stamm, Jeff Gentry, Lovelace Cook, Karena de Souza, John Hollenbeck, Kelly Woods, Annette Mason, and Trent Selbrede for being with me on the journey. You are the best group of writers I could ever have hoped for. I adore all of you – but most especially, my 'just outside of Boston' buddy and friend, Win Treese.

It is with unspeakable joy to share my ideas and process with you. I do hope it helps. As a first-time author, I'm sure I missed things that you need. I am here for you as you adopt these ideas. You'll find more templates, workshop materials, examples, and contact information at www.YourMessagingSucks.com.

Index

A

B

C

D

E

F

I

M

O

P

R

S

V

W

CPSIA information can be obtained
at www.ICGtesting.com
Printed in the USA
LVHW071315120323
741435LV00008B/189/J